LIVING WITH
A DEAD MAN
a story of love

EMERALD LAKE
BOOKS

Books published by Emerald Lake Books may be ordered through booksellers or by contacting:

Emerald Lake Books
44 Green Pond Rd
Sherman, CT 06784
http://emeraldlakebooks.com
860-946-0544

ISBN: 978-0-9965674-2-8 (pb)
ISBN: 978-0-9965674-3-5 (epub)

Printed in the United States of America

This poignant memoir chronicles the journey of Marianne Bette's family as they struggled with the impending death of a much loved husband and father, a death and dying therapist. Marianne's story is told with sensitivity and raw honesty, sharing her personal thoughts, feelings and struggles as well as her young children's reactions. She reveals her own vulnerabilities as she describes both the good and not so good times as she faced the challenges of being a wife, mother and doctor. Her account of this journey is candid and insightful. After reading it you are likely to view both life and death differently. I encourage everyone to read *Living with a Dead Man*, not just those facing the death of a loved one.

Carol Flament, M.S., SPHR, SHRM-SCP
Death, Dying and Bereavement educator and
Bereavement Support Group Facilitator

Death and dying are serious businesses, but not entirely grim businesses. Within them can be found humor, warmth and, most importantly, love. *Living With a Dead Man* made me laugh, made me cry and left me hopeful. It is a celebration of intertwined lives well lived, well loved and well ended.

Craig W. Czarsty, M.D.
Former Board Chair, American Board of Family Medicine

As long as we're all going to die, why don't we learn to do it really, really well? Marianne Bette invites you on a journey that will carry you from the depths of heartbreak to the heights of celebration. Accept the invitation. Come and discover that dying has very little to do with death and everything to do with life. This is a discovery that could change your dying some day in the future, but can truly change your living today.

Rev. Dr. Bonnie Bardot
Retired Pastor, United Church of Christ

To anyone who is facing the ending of a life,
be it their own or that of a loved one.

May you not fear death,
but be grateful for the gift of time—
time to live, laugh, and love,
and time to celebrate
and enjoy every day.

Contents

Introduction 1

The Beginning 3

The Diagnosis 25

Treatment Options 39

The Family 45

Sarah's Story 53

Living With Cancer 63

The Blessing Known as "Bob" 77

The Drumming Begins 85

Fuck Cancer 89

The Truth 93

The Realization 105

The Conversation 119

Life After Hope Is Gone 131

Dying Man's Power 137

The In-Laws 145

More Visitors 157

It Takes a Village 165

Reconciliation 175

The End Is Near 179

The Morning After 191

The Service 201

The End 209

Author's Note 215

Acknowledgements 217

About the Author 219

Introduction

The reason you are holding this book in your hands, my dear, is because I wrote it for you.

Although I am not a writer, I do have a lot of experience with death and dying as a family physician, and more importantly I have a great story to tell.

This story is about my husband, Thom's, last year of life and how we all went through it—Thom, myself, our children, extended family, friends and community.

Our experiences were moving, enlightening and funny at times (really), which compelled me to write about them.

Unfortunately, the concepts of death and dying are still cloaked in fear, secrets and unknowns. They can overwhelm and unravel the most even-tempered person. (Maybe we are supposed to fall apart. How else could we integrate such a dramatic change into our lives?)

Yet death is our common destination—the one event we will all share.

Throughout this book, you'll find quotations from my patients as well. Perhaps their thoughts will resonate with you as much as they did with me.

My hope is that by reading this memoir you will feel our connectedness and recognize our similarities, and that it reduces your fears, opens your heart and mind, and reminds you that you are not alone.

Most of all I hope you will recognize the incredible opportunities that can occur when someone has time to say "goodbye."

The Beginning

"You think it's forever. There ain't nothing forever except death. Death is forever." – Vincent McCauley

Thom had his seizure at the end of Justine's second grade parent/teacher conference.

In that moment, he careened off the path of a contented life into the unknown and took all of us with him: me, our three daughters (Caitlin, Justine and Sarah) and everyone we knew. There have been many beginnings and endings in my life, but none as dramatic as this—the beginning of the end of my husband.

Justine was the catalyst for our move from California back to Connecticut three years earlier. She was only three months old when we had a drive-by shooting in our town, in the desert outside of Los Angeles.

Nothing of this magnitude had happened in our community before and everyone was rattled by this senseless violent act. It came on the heels of another tragedy only a month before, when the valedictorian of the local high school was killed in gang-related violence.

After those two events, Justine practically lived in a baby carrier strapped to my chest. Somehow I felt she was safest when she was close to my heart.

Three days after the shooting, I was waiting my turn in line at the bank when a question occurred to me. *Where would I go in this bank to protect my child if someone drives by right now and starts shooting?*

I found myself analyzing the thickness of the concrete walls and pillars for their ability to protect my daughter from bullets. I could stand behind this one, or I could dive behind that one. They would probably do the job.

My awareness of this thought process scared the hell out of me. I know all mothers have the "she-bear" instinct to protect their child, but actually spending mental energy on ways to dodge bullets? No way. It was time to move.

To say that Thom was shocked about my idea of moving is putting it lightly.

"You want to move?" he asked in an odd, high-pitched voice. "To—-?"

He left the question hanging, as if the only place left was with the shrub brush and tumbleweeds.

"It's not to. It's from," I answered.

"You want to move out of our house?" He spoke like a person who had just had a stroke and has to concentrate to form his thoughts. "You want to move out of town?"

"I want to move out of California." I spoke slowly so his stroke-mind would get it.

I understood his resistance. Thom was a native Californian. His parents and brothers lived in California. He had a thriving psychotherapy practice of 28 years in Hollywood with a second office in Lancaster for 12 of those years. All our friends lived in California. I had a successful 18-year-old family practice that I started from scratch and had never been happier with my work, my patients or the doctors with whom I worked. Plus, I had just been awarded "Doctor of the Year" by the local paper.

This move would be financial suicide. Our colleagues were flabbergasted. No one walks away from rewarding, well-oiled, financially secure, professional careers like we had, no one—and certainly not at the mid-point of their careers. But that's exactly what we did. The only explanation we had, and granted some people never did get it, was that it was a metaphysical decision.

It took about three years to orchestrate. First, we had to figure out where we were going. Then when. Then how.

Owning land on a river in Connecticut was a big draw. The property was bordered on three sides by the National Audubon Society, which meant that our house would be on a tongue of property embedded in a pristine forest filled with birds. For all intents and purposes, we would not have any neighbors. It seemed ideal to me.

Thom was not too crazy about moving to Connecticut, but somehow he became convinced. Perhaps it was the excitement of building our own house. Or maybe it was the fact that he and I had gone to prep schools in the East, and we wanted our daughters to have the same type of education we dearly valued.

Plus, my parents were getting older, and I felt the need to be there for them, especially my mother. Somewhere in the core of my being, I knew I was supposed to be there for her death and dying time.

But what I remember most about those discussions is when he asked me, "Where would you want to be with the girls if something happened to me?"

My knee-jerk response was, "Connecticut. I would have a large support system there."

He simply nodded several times, as if pondering what my life would be like without him to support me and the girls. I didn't think any more about it except that it was a cute thought.

We tried to look at the positives of the move. Thom had the most to lose, leaving his family and a practice that was a big part of who he was. He loved psychotherapy and was outrageously good at it.

During those last years in California, he started to focus more on death, dying and grief. Patients who had lost a loved one or a body part to cancer, like a breast, had a lot of adjustments to make and Thom could talk them through it.

Relationships lost through divorce, death and separation were easy for him. But people dying or facing death were his favorite. "They really want to move spiritually," he would say, as if he were talking about something exciting.

The toughest patient he ever had was a man that accidentally ran over and killed his own toddler on Father's Day. Honestly, I don't know how Thom did it, but over time he helped that man pull his life together and function like a human being again.

Yeah, Thom was a good therapist... a really good one.

He said that after 28 years, he was ready to retire from his general practice to become a death and dying therapist. He thought a small practice in an office in our house would suit him just fine. I would be the wage-earner and he would be the house husband with a part-time practice. We agreed that would be the perfect way to slip into the second half of our lives.

It was nearly true. He did help me run my practice when we got to Connecticut and he did see a small number of patients (though not limited to death and dying). Overall, we were pretty content.

The day of his seizure, we had blocked our afternoon schedules for Justine's conference. In the five-minute drive from our office to her school, Thom commented that Justine could yet be the brightest one in our family—such a happy thought.

As we pulled into the parking lot, I noticed how different the school looked now, compared to my years there in grade school. The old brick building had pods of portable classrooms branching out in different directions like articulated crab legs.

We entered through the old original hallway. Then there was a subtle shift in the long hallway to Justine's "portable." The solid floor of vinyl tiles gave way to carpeted plywood floor. They felt and sounded hollow beneath our feet. The walls of large shiny blond bricks, so popular back in the '50s, gave way to sheetrock walls that were lined by slender metal lockers on metal feet.

Too slender to hide in, I thought, remembering my second grade antics.

Her classroom had a familiarity to it. It was bright and airy, with five or six long windows looking out to the west. Through the windows and down a grassy slope, you could see the new playground equipment donated by the PTA.

Justine's favorites were the tire swing and the monkey bars, even though they initially caused her hands to blister and peel. She spent at least half of her recess upside down.

Inside the classroom, there were cozy clusters of four to six desks in different parts of the room. On top of each blond fake-wood desk was a child's name laminated in large, perfectly printed block letters, taped over the indentation of the pencil holder.

Even without seeing her name, I could have picked out Justine's desk from across the room. Her desk top was scrubbed shiny clean. The gray metal drawer that hung underneath held her neatly stacked books from largest to smallest. It was a testament not only to her love of order, but also her love of her school and teachers.

Justine stood proudly next to her desk, straight, tall and relaxed. Her long black hair, so much like her Dad's, hung in waves to her waist. She fixed her twinkling dark-brown eyes on us as we approached her from the doorway. Her long fingers held her folder of selected works from the year.

"Okay, Mom and Dad," she directed. "Please sit down. After Ms. Little talks to you for a few minutes, I am going to take over and present my second grade folder to you so you can see how far I have come." She sounded so official.

We sat down at Justine's cluster of desks. She and I sat on one side and Thom sat across from us.

Looking at him as Justine opened her folder, I noticed that he was more handsome now that his full head of wavy black hair was almost half gray. "Salt and pepper," my mother used to call it.

His dark brown eyes could have a piercing quality at times and his left eyebrow had an old scar in it that caused a slight tenting to the brow as if he was always contemplating a question. The tenting vanished when he smiled as he did now and then winked to let me know he thought this was going to be fun.

Thom and I sat with our knees sticking up over the low desk tops. We were two big people in her smaller world. This was her space, her school, her work, her teacher and she was proud of them. The full manila folder lay open on her desk and before us was stacked Justine's full year of written work.

"This is how I wrote at the beginning of the year," she said, showing us a piece of her earlier work. "And this is how I write *now*." She proudly presented her last story.

Thom and I carefully read and commented, not only on her penmanship, spelling and sentence structure, but also on the obvious progression in her ability to write a good story.

Thom and I exchanged that parental "knowing look." Justine was bright and full of promise—her writing made that clear. As I read through more of her work, I started to think he was probably right about her smart potential.

Suddenly Thom exclaimed, "Marianne! What's happening to me?"

He extended his left arm straight out in front of his chest as if for me to examine it. His hand hung oddly askew from his wrist. His thumb and the first two fingers were contracting and relaxing in a quick rhythmical fashion as if he were making an "okay sign," even though things were clearly *not okay*.

Without looking at his face, I might have thought he was teasing and acting goofy, as he often did. But his face held a mixture of shock and dismay, and his voice held an emotion I had never heard from him before. Fear.

In that split second, everything in my mind came to a screeching halt. I tried to comprehend the bizarre situation before me. Time stopped for an unbelievably few wide seconds—or perhaps my thoughts just moved faster than the speed of light.

Immediately my mind splintered into three parts: the wife, the mother and the doctor. They were all *on*. Full speed. Racing down parallel tracks.

The wife wanted to stand up and scream, "No. No! No, this can't be happening. This is my husband. Oh my God, my husband. My husband is having a seizure. *No!*"

I could imagine the repercussions of that scream. I could envision the teacher and other students with their parents running over from their desks, everyone standing there looking at Thom having his seizure.

The mother in me wanted to protect Justine from that scene. Screaming would freak her out and embarrass her at the same time. It would be too much for her to handle. That was not an option.

Ultimately, it was the doctor in me that took over. I immediately concluded that there would be no reason for Thom to have a seizure except that he had a tumor growing in his head. It would be pressing on nerve cells and setting off abnormal cell connections, causing nerves to fire and trigger muscles to contract involuntarily.

The doctor continued to assess the situation. Start with the basics. He is breathing. He is alert. His heart is fine.

So, time the seizure. Track its course. It might be important in the diagnosis. I looked at my watch as I thought about this type of seizure, which marches up a limb in a contracting and relaxing fashion. It is a Jacksonian seizure. I had learned about them in med school but had never witnessed one before. *How odd*, I thought, *to see my first one in my own husband.*

The three of us sat transfixed watching as the seizure climbed up Thom's left wrist and then his arm. Pinching fingers, flexing wrist, muscles tensing then relaxing in his arm. Then the left side of his face began contracting in rhythm with his left eye, which was flying open and squeezing shut while the lower part of his face and mouth tightened and relaxed in a lopsided grimace.

Thom looked at me aghast and pleaded for an explanation. "What is happening to me?"

The wife thought, "Oh, honey. We are in real trouble."

The mother thought, "Don't freak out the child."

The doctor was timing the progress of the Jacksonian seizure. It lasted 15, maybe 20, seconds.

All three minds were on high alert, all thinking, but not speaking.

"Mom!" Justine elbowed me in the side and added in that wake-up kind of tone, "Dad is having a seizure."

"Yes, Justine. You are right, but it's okay now. It's starting to fade." *How did she know it was a seizure?*

Thom started to relax. I grabbed my cell phone and dialed the imaging center in town and asked for the manager.

"Chris, this is Doctor Bette. I need your help. My husband just had a seizure. Can we come over right now for a CT scan of his head?"

The doctor in me was sure the first thing to do was to get a picture of the brain and see if anything was growing in there.

As we left her classroom, Justine and I walked on either side of Thom like bodyguards.

There was now a fourth dimension to my thinking. My viewpoint had totally shifted. I felt completely outside of my body, out of space, out of time and definitely out of my mind.

I felt like I was looking at my life as an outsider or as if I was sitting in the audience watching a movie, not connected to the present at all. My new viewpoint was from the ceiling over the lockers, watching the three of us walk down the hall.

The wife in me was in shock.

The mother was checking in on Justine and making sure she was as unaffected as possible.

The doctor was hard at work, firing off a million doctor-type questions that Thom answered in monotones and monosyllables.

"Can you walk okay?"

"Yes."

"Do you feel any numbness or weakness in your arms or legs?"

"No."

"Can you see okay? Do you notice any vision changes?"

"Yes. No."

"Have you had anything like this before?"

"No."

"Are you fatigued anywhere?"

He thinks, then answers, "No."

"Did you know this was coming on?"

"No."

"Do you have a headache?"

"No."

Thom knew that the doctor in me was checking him out, which appeared to make him feel slightly better. I observed his ability to walk. He looked perfectly well-balanced and physically unaffected by what had just happened.

His comprehension was acutely normal, his responses appropriate. He seemed completely intact both mentally and physically.

Thank God, the wife chimed in.

But somehow I was still in that disconnected place, watching from afar, not feeling a thing. From my ceiling perspective, I saw us moving along the hall toward the front door.

Something about the sunshine hitting me was like a chemical reaction. *Pow!* I reconnected to the here and now and snapped back into my body.

I remember getting into Thom's Range Rover, but I remember little of the drive to the imaging center. Chris met us at the door and ushered Thom right into the scanner.

In the waiting room, Justine and I sat on the edge of our chairs and hugged and rocked each other for... I don't know how long.

Slowly, I began to regain my consciousness. I noticed other people in the waiting room as if they had just appeared. A few people were staring at us. A few were pretending that they weren't.

"What is going to happen to Daddy?" I knew Justine needed her mother, not the doctor. The kid was only seven years old and had just watched her Dad have a seizure. She needed her Mom. She needed reassurance.

"Well, they will do a CT scan of his head and then we will find out why he had a seizure." I said this as matter-of-factly as I possibly could.

"Is he going to be alright?" she asked with her brow furrowed and a piercing intensity in her eyes.

He may have something awful so you can't lie, the doctor in me warned.

No, but you have to be hopeful and let her digest things a little at a time, the mother replied.

I faced her squarely. You simply cannot sugar-coat a seizure. "I honestly don't know, Justine. We have to wait and see what Chris finds on the scan, okay?"

Justine already knew much of the reality of life and death. We had always allowed her and her sister, Caitlin, to hear the stories of our patients.

She knew about cancer and death—at least from arm's length. She had accompanied me on rounds in the hospital and seen people on machines and IVs. Things that would have scared the average child seemed more familiar to her by sheer exposure. Patients would often show her their incisions and scars from surgery. She thought it was actually neat when she could see the staples that were often used instead of sutures.

Chris came out to the waiting room. "Dr. Bette, would you please come in?"

Justine clung to my arm and pleaded, "Mom, don't leave me here in the waiting room by myself."

The doctor in me said, *If you take her in, she is going to hear the diagnosis and then you won't be able to control the information.* But the mother in me could not leave my child in the waiting room alone and scared. Not only would she feel abandoned, but the fear of the unknown can be worse to a child than the reality of cancer.

I knew how strong-willed Justine was and, if I tried to leave her with someone else, she would have raised a big stink and made the whole situation that much more difficult. So I grabbed her hand and headed into the back office where the scanners were.

My radiologist colleague was peering into the blue-white x-ray view box where there were many "cuts" or pictures at different levels of Thom's brain.

"Hi, Paulo," I said. "What's he got?"

He clicked on one of the pictures to enlarge it.

"He has a small brain tumor here," he pointed to a tiny white dot in the picture of the left side of his brain. "The rest looks clear."

Looking closely at that little white dot, the wife in me asked how such a small thing could cause such a big reaction in a person's body. But as my face bathed in the light of the viewing screen, the doctor took over.

Okay, it's small and well-circumscribed. At least it's not one of those oligodendrogliomas. Those are inoperable, or the operation never seems to get it all due to the way it grows in tentacles. This at least looked like it could be cut out. Eliminated. But what type of a tumor was it? Afraid of the answer, I asked Paulo.

He answered softly. "It's not a primary brain tumor. It's a met."

He meant that this tumor came from somewhere else and traveled, or metastasized, to the head. The doctor in me thought, *Oh, shit. If it has already travelled, he has at least two tumors. It is not contained. Oh boy, this is going to be one bad deal...*

"Do you know where the primary might be?" Paulo asked softly.

"Check his lungs," I said immediately. "He used to be a heavy smoker."

I was immediately transported back to the last argument I had with Thom, about six months earlier, when I again found a cigarette lighter in his pocket while putting his pants in the washing machine. Furious with him, it actually started a screaming match between us in our bathroom.

I told him if he was going to die of lung cancer and leave me to raise these two girls by myself, I wasn't even going to attend his funeral. Holy shit! *How did I know?*

The chest x-ray revealed a small tumor in his left lung. "You may as well do a CT scan of the chest too," I suggested, knowing we would have to find out how involved the lungs were.

The doctor was done. The diagnosis was made. The work-up was nearly complete.

The wife, however, could see the sad look on Paulo's face as he watched me absorb the reality of my husband's cancer. It's a diagnosis all doctors hate to make, but having to tell it to your colleague is that much more difficult. I touched his arm lightly in a nonverbal thanks as I left to tell Thom what we'd found.

Justine and I were back in the waiting room, hugging each other again as we waited for the thirty-minute scan of his chest to be completed.

Suddenly I remembered my other daughter, Caitlin. What the hell happened to me? How could I forget my own daughter or maybe it was a miracle that I did remember? I was supposed to pick Caitlin up after Justine's conference. She was waiting for us back at my office. I quickly checked the time. An hour had gone by at the imaging center. It was one of the longest hours of my life.

"Justine, let's go get Caitlin. She is at the office waiting to get picked up."

"Mom, I am not leaving Dad here by himself," she stated emphatically.

"He will be here with Chris and the doctor."

"Mom!" It was clear she was not budging, so Chris agreed to keep an eye on her. As I was leaving I heard Chris ask if she wanted to go inside and watch her Dad get scanned. They went back to the scanner hand-in-hand.

A few minutes later, parked in front of my office, I could see Caitlin through the glass door. She was in the front office engrossed in copying her bibliography for the upcoming National History Day competition.

The doctor in me was steeling her nerves.

The wife was totally bereft.

The mother was heartbroken.

I know I am about to deliver the worst news of her life. *How am I going to do that? Why aren't there instruction manuals for the really hard parts of life? Okay, think.* I couldn't leave out any important detail that Justine would be sure to tell her later.

As I contemplated how and what to say, as well as what not to say, I sat there watching my 13-year-old daughter through the window.

Right now, she was free of the reality I was bearing. I wanted a few more minutes, God I never wanted to deliver this news to her, but right now I wanted to drink in her innocence. I wanted that mental picture to stick in my mind, the one of her pain-free and cancer-free.

For those few precious moments, my fractionated mind was put on hold as I observed my classic Irish beauty at work. Her intensity, paired with her graceful movements, was mesmerizing. Her long brown wavy hair, shot full of copper highlights, moved over her shoulders as she collated her work.

As she moved back and forth between the counter she was working at and the copy machine, her round glasses caught the glare of the overhead lights. Although I couldn't see her hazel eyes, I could easily recall their twinkle and that contagious smile of hers revealing her chipped front tooth.

Caitlin was an excellent student. Last year, in seventh grade, she had gotten totally enthralled in a history project that led her to compete in National History Day. She and her friend performed a live re-enactment of the First Amendment (freedom of the press) and they won first place in the state and went on to compete nationally in the finals in Maryland.

My daughter loved the competition and therefore did another live performance, by herself this year, on the 13th and 14th amendments (prohibition and the repeal of prohibition). Once again, she won first place in the state and was on her way to compete with all the other 50 state's top winners.

Thom was supposed to drive her to Maryland and be her support parent. That was no longer an option… More bad news.

My heart was pounding in my throat as I entered my office and then took her hands in mine. The doctor-mind and mother-mind melded together to relate to this sweet child. "Honey, I have something really difficult to tell you. Something happened to Dad today."

As I recounted the occurrences of the last few hours, Caitlin took it all in silently. The tears rolled unchecked under her glasses and over her freckled cheeks. Her pain and vulnerability rolled up together and hit me like a bowling ball in the center of my chest.

How quickly she comprehended the gravity of her Dad's seizure and brain tumor. She looked imploringly at me as she wept. Would I please tell her this wasn't true?

Thirteen is a tender age, but to lose a parent of the opposite sex at that developmental stage could be devastating. I had seen adolescents in the lock-up psych ward who had "lost it" under similar situations. Would that happen to my Caitlin? *No*, I thought, *too solid*.

Caitlin had an incredible foundation in her life. She also had a joy and love for life that was part of her from Day One. Nope, this kid would be okay if anyone would be in a situation like this.

"Mom, does this mean that Dad is going to die?" Right to the point.

Every word was so important. What was said and how it was said had to be consistent with the way we raised our children. Honest. Considerate. Hopeful.

"We don't know yet, honey. First and foremost, Dad feels fine and is in no danger of dying at the moment." I spoke each sentence slowly enough and watched her face to see it register. "He has no headache. He is not short of breath or anything like that, and the cancer is small."

Don't paint too rosy a picture, the doctor chimed in.

"But having it in two places is not a good sign. We just have to go through this one step at a time. There are different types of lung cancer. We have to figure out which one he has so we can figure out the best way to treat it. Dad is young and has no other medical problems. These are on his side."

I tried to project a hope that the doctor in me did not feel. But both the mother and the doctor knew the incredible importance of hope, especially at this point.

When we arrived back at the imaging center, everyone in the office seemed to look the other way or become engrossed in their paperwork. It must have been very painful to anyone who knew us to look at the shock in our expressions and know what was going wrong in our lives.

Thom, sitting on the scanner table, consoled Justine and Caitlin as I spoke to Paulo.

"Okay, Marianne. There's just the one small tumor in the chest, which is the primary, plus the small 'met' in the head." Paulo went silent, giving me time to process. He didn't realize, of course, that the wife and mother in me were listening to my girls and their Dad, even as the doctor in me took in the news.

I squinted really hard at that spot on the scan. Okay he was a heavy smoker before I met him, but he had stopped. Well, I guess he started and stopped a hundred times or more. Damn it. Adding up all those pack-years, the accumulation was against him. He never even had a cough or shortness of breath. In fact, he could swim the length of the pool underwater and often commented about how good his lung capacity was. He never got any lung infections and never took any antibiotics.

The wife interjected, *Maybe he has a pretty good immune system after all.*

The doctor replied, *He's got **lung cancer** for God's sake.*

Immediately, I thought of all the patients I'd had with lung and brain cancers. I could see their faces, their diagnostic work-ups, their treatments, their surgeries and their chemotherapies. Some of them made it. Most of them didn't.

What course were we on here with Thom? Would he have surgery and chemo and be one of the lucky ones?

The drive home was in deafening silence. I never even noticed the natural beauty that always struck me in the S-shaped driveway. Rhododendron bushes backed up by hemlocks, maples and birch trees. The house plays peek-a-boo through the trees until the first turn when a large cedar and stone house is revealed in the middle of a forest.

Almost every trip down the driveway, I would pause there for a second to appreciate the beauty of it all. But not today. I noticed nothing, as if the canvas of my life had been erased.

At home, the four of us sat shell-shocked on the couch. Thom had a girl glued to each hip, and they were hugging him as if the closer they could get to him the more they could insulate him or themselves from the cancer. We were all drawing comfort from the physical contact of our bodies touching.

Thom told the girls that he was fine now and that once they figured out the best way to treat the cancer, he would be on the road to a cure. The mother and wife were going right along with those thoughts and reassurances.

It seemed like everyone's anxiety came down about five notches. Everyone's except the doctor's. I knew it would not be that easy. I would need all the help I could get to get him on a treatment program. That meant talking to my good friend the oncologist, Kert.

Kert had cared for my mother when she had colon cancer. My understanding and respect for him grew as he cared for her through the entire process. Together the three of us went through the diagnosis, the surgery, the chemotherapy, the complications and finally her decision to stop all treatment and "let cancer have its way with me," as she said.

He was supportive of her death as well. He was one of the all-too-rare compassionate and loving physicians. Without a doubt, there was no one I wanted to talk to more in that moment than Kert.

"I know he is not on call, but I want to speak to him anyway," I insisted to the woman at his answering service. I started pacing the atrium of our house, where I had gone to have this private conversation.

"No, I do *not* want to talk to the doctor on call. I only want to speak to Kert." I was losing my patience and was afraid my sanity would be next. "Look, I am sorry if I am being demanding here, but I am a colleague of his. My husband had a seizure this afternoon and has just been diagnosed with cancer. I need to speak with him and only him. Please, just page him. I know he will call me back as soon as he gets the message."

I waited, pacing, pacing... As I tried to calm myself down, I peeked around the side of the stone fireplace and saw Thom and the girls still sitting on the green velvet couch. I heard the hum of their voices and, although I couldn't hear exactly what was being said, I could see that Thom was talking slowly and deliberately, answering each of their questions. I knew that he was using this technique to calm the girls. I also knew that pretty soon he would be teasing them, they would be laughing, and the situation would be diffused for the moment.

As I returned to my pacing, my mind traveled back to the spouses of my cancer patients. Immediately, I connected with their gut feelings of shock, dismay and panic. Their feelings were as clear as if they were tattooed across their forehead.

Cancer. My spouse has cancer. *Our life is over.*

That word was stamped on every thought, every action, every dream, every cell in their body: CANCER.

I was connected to them as their doctor, of course, but now I was connected as a person, just like them... a person in love with someone who could die.

Quite suddenly I was initiated into the Cancer Club, the membership I never wanted. The one that immediately transformed me into a different person in a different reality. I could never go back to what it was like without the impact of that word in my life. My choices had evaporated right along with life as I had known it. Forever and ever.

Kert called back and I told him the story. He agreed to see both of us the following afternoon. There was nothing more my doctor brain could do at the moment.

I had been right. The girls were more relaxed and the conversation was drifting onto other topics. They had been convinced he was okay for now. They were able to let go of him and eventually move out of the room. Thom was sitting there and I quickly slipped right in next to him. It was finally time for husband and wife.

I took his hand in mine and kissed it and brought it to my cheek. Teary eyes locked onto each other as we digested the weight of the day's events. Silent communication. Somehow, here in our own home, on our own couch, without the x-rays and technicians and kids, reality was sinking in. Really sinking in.

I was sinking. Suddenly I felt a heavy hot wave wash over me. *He is sitting here with me now, but he could be gone tomorrow,* I thought.

My mouth went dry as I swallowed back bitter bile and took several shallow breaths.

I flashed back to my first fiancé, Kerry. At 33 years old, I had never been so happy. Kerry owned a small plane, but was selling it because he wanted to buy a bigger one. He decided to take the plane up for one last flight before he said goodbye. When he returned from his flight, we would go shopping in Los Angeles for our wedding rings. But he didn't return. Not alive. His plane crashed, and he—and my dreams—were gone in a flash.

How lost, scared and ill-prepared I was, even as a 33-year-old doctor, to face that death. It took me years to find my way back from wherever that tragedy had sent me. There were a million questions and no answers. How I wish I had been able to ask him certain things before he died. Maybe it would have helped me in the aftermath.

Before I knew what was happening, I felt this tremendous compulsion to start asking Thom questions. They flew out of me like arrows shot by an archer in rapid succession without any thought other than to hit the target before it was gone.

"Will I have to sell the house?"

"Can I survive financially without you?"

"Did we cancel all the life insurance policies when we were avoiding bankruptcy or just some of them?"

"Do I need to put the house in my name alone?"

"The cars? They are in both our names, right?"

"Are our wills up to date?"

"Can I afford to send the girls to college?"

Thom sat there quietly answering each question as each arrow stuck its target. Suddenly, I stopped just as quickly as I had begun when I finally noticed the effect they were having on him.

His face was white. His jaw was tense and he looked shot.

"Oh my God, Thom, I am so sorry. It's just—I couldn't help thinking back to Kerry. I was so lost then. So lost. For too long. I can't go there again, to that dark oppressive place. Choked. Overwhelmed. Emotionally shut down and shut off. So depressed for so long. I know I can't survive if I have to do that again. Now I've got the girls to think of. I've got to be more together for them… Oh my God, Thom, I can't do it without you." I sobbed and hung onto Thom for dear life, as if he would be safe if I held him close to my heart.

"I know, honey. It's scary, but I am going to be okay," he said softly petting my hair and patting my back.

"But it doesn't *feel* okay. It feels awful, like before you puke. You know you are going to, but you think if you don't move maybe it won't happen."

He continued petting me and trying to help me settle down.

"You are such a part of me. Of my life. Our life. Our family. How could I ever survive without you? How am I going to get my head right? Oh Thom, how are we going to do this?"

"We are going to take it one step at a time, honey." He spoke as if he had been through this before. "Right now, I feel fine. We will go to Kert tomorrow. He'll figure out how to kill this stuff. Then I'll be alright. I'm young. Aside from this, I am healthy."

Everything he said I knew to be true in my mind, but my life and my heart were broken. I wanted everything that he said to be true, especially the part about him eventually being all right. I really wanted that part to be true. But every doctor cell in my body was saying, *Don't buy it. He's not going to make it.*

I felt as if I were going to go crazy thinking one way as a doctor and another as a wife and mother. Worst of all, I knew that the doctor was right.

"As far as the girls and our life here at home goes," he began, pausing in that way of his that always let me know he was thinking this through as he spoke. "I want it to be as normal as possible, change as little as we can. Let it all settle into a new routine."

I wondered how that could happen—settling into a routine with cancer. Generally, I thought it was a good idea, but could I act "normal" while I had a belly full of impending doom?

"So let me get this straight, honey." I was trying to recap and regroup. "We are going to act normal while we deal with your cancer?"

I asked this as if it was an unbelievable script he was asking me to follow, like drinking poison and pretending it's Kool-Aid.

"Right, as much as we possibly can."

Since I had no alternate plan and it was his cancer, I figured we may as well play it his way.

"If that's what you want, that's what we'll do. You're probably right. You usually are."

In that moment it seemed to me that I was going to need a fairly large dose of denial to get through this.

"I think it is a fairly good plan," he continued.

I was trying to get myself to agree.

"But, honey," he began.

"Yeah?"

"You have to do me one really big favor."

Wanting to please him more than anything in the world, I replied, "Sure, honey, anything. You name it. What do you want?"

"You have to stop looking at me as if you are living with a dead man."

The Diagnosis

"Cancer changes everything. Forever and forever." – *Marty Ludorf,*
with three close family members with breast cancer

Sitting in an oncologist's waiting room is one of life's more sobering experiences. The first thing that hit me was that I was there, not as a doctor, but as a cancer patient's wife.

Cancer patient.

Those two words are one big mouthful.

Kert's waiting room was rather unimaginative. The room was lined on either side with chairs. Each one, I noted, had arm rests to help frail people to get up. Occasional end tables were covered with old magazines. Boxed fluorescent lighting shone from the ceiling.

The receptionist sat behind a window busily working on a computer. When she told us to have a seat, Thom and I each grabbed a magazine and headed to the far end of the waiting room.

We were sitting near a large fake plant that was supposed to look like ornamental grass. I was thinking that if it was real it might be able to give some sort of comfort to the people around it. But where would it get its light? Were there any nurturing souls there that would care for it? I guessed a plastic plant was better than no plant or worse yet a dead one. Maybe someday I would talk to Kert about this.

As I sat with an outdated issue of People Magazine in my lap, I looked around the room with my doctor-mind at work.

Across from us was an older couple sitting side-by-side, quietly reading.

He looked like an average healthy 70-year-old man. He had mostly white to gray hair, glasses, tanned skin, mildly arthritic hands, a beige zipper jacket, chinos and deck shoes.

His wife (I assumed) had one of those head wrap scarves on her head. She had no hair sticking out like you would expect at the temples or nape of her neck and she was striking in her paleness. Her face was white, her hands were white, and her neck was white. Anemia, I diagnosed. Doubtless, a result of the chemo. Color and *joie de vivre* are the first to go. She was dressed for winter, even though it was mid-May.

Maybe she is going to get a unit of blood today, I thought. I hoped so because she would look and feel a lot better then. Now, she looked as if she was being erased.

To their right was another couple, obviously mother and daughter. The mother looked quite similar to the pale lady except she was older and more feeble. She seemed as if she had lost her way. She was confused and undone in her manner, her speech and her dress, and she looked like she had just rolled out of bed.

The daughter sat next to her with a clipboard on her lap. It had a number of papers on it, a list of questions and lab results. She seemed irritated with her mother. I wondered what their relationship was usually like. What happened to make her so out of sorts? Is her mother getting worse? Is the mother leaning too heavily on the daughter? Is she the caretaker? Maybe the daughter is getting burned out herself?

On our side of the room were two women. One had very short hair—growing in after chemo, or so it seemed. She actually looked pretty good. Although I couldn't hear what they were saying, the conversation seemed animated and she gave off this attitude like, "I survived the chemo and beat the cancer, and I am here to get the good news."

Boy, I sure hope so. Her companion had a hopeful look too. Who is she? The sister? They don't look alike... maybe her partner or best friend.

Which cancer did she beat? Breast cancer, I assume. *Go, girl. Someone's got to win sometime.*

Another patient entered the waiting room holding a stainless steel bowl (known as a "throw-up pan" at our house). They go right in. No waiting room time for them, thank goodness.

At the other end of the waiting room, there was a middle-aged man reading by himself. He was probably picking someone up after their chemo. He would be the driver.

There was an empty chair between him and the next man who also looked pretty healthy. He was about 65 and had all his hair, his color was good and his face looked bright. I wondered how he fit in here, in the oncologist's waiting room.

As I scanned his clothes, I saw it. The little plastic tubing sticking out of the end of his red plaid sleeve. Yep, him too. He was here for chemo. He was probably just starting since he looked so good. It usually takes two or three rounds before hair falls out and anemia sets in.

A round middle-aged lady in scrubs called our names, interrupting my doctoral review of the waiting room and bringing me back to my own reality. "The doctor is running behind, but you can sit and wait in his office."

I felt as if a temporary reprieve had been granted.

The assistant gave us the office tour. Immediately inside the door on the right was the blood drawing room. On the left was the scale, just like in my office, but it had a completely different significance in an oncologist's office where cancer patients struggle to maintain their weight.

As we turned right down the hallway to Kert's office, we passed by a large open room with lots of windows. It was filled with eight or ten La-Z-Boy recliners. Half of the seats were occupied by people attached by clear plastic tubing to bags hung on IV poles.

Some people were watching television. Others were sleeping under colorful hand-crocheted blankets like my grandmother made. One pale man was reclining with his eyes closed and earphones plugged in. I wondered if listening to classical music would reduce the nausea that often goes along with the chemo.

"This is our chemo room," the assistant said proudly. "People usually stay here for a few hours. They can read or sleep or even bring in their own DVDs to watch."

She said it cheerfully, like they were great choices. My doctor head was noting how it all worked, but my wife head was wondering how my husband will feel, sitting there watching TV in a room-full of people he doesn't know, who are all getting poison pumped into their veins that makes them feel like throwing up.

We waited in Kert's office, walking around, looking at his pictures and diplomas. We were way too nervous to sit. Soon, Kert came bustling in and apologized for being late, as if he hadn't squeezed us into his already full schedule. His small frame and stature belied the articulate, insightful and empathetic giant I know him to be.

In his office, he had that professional look and attitude that lets you know he means business—quite a different view from the impish, playful Kert that my call partner, Craig, and I get together with for the occasional drink on a Friday night. In that one hour of unwinding, we would catch up on each other's kids, travels and good books recently read.

I knew from those conversations that Kert loves to cycle, cook and spend time with his wife, with whom he is madly in love even after 25 years of marriage. But that was not the man I saw before me. We were here to see the doctor, not the friend I know and love.

He pulled the two chairs from in front of his desk and placed them side-by-side in the middle of the room. Then he rolled his desk chair around to face the two chairs.

"Please sit down," he said gesturing for Thom and me to sit facing him.

"I came in early this morning and reviewed your scans myself. Then I went over them with the neuroradiologist I respect the most. I also spoke with the interventional radiologist about what has to happen next. But before I go into all this, Thom can you tell me exactly what happened to you yesterday?"

Kert has this incredible ability to focus on you in a way that lets you know you have his total concentration. As Thom related his story, Kert never took his eyes off Thom. Clearly, I was not the focus.

My doctor head was happy that a connection was being established between the doctor and patient, not the patient's doctor-spouse.

When Thom was finished, Kert summarized the situation. "This looks like a small lung cancer in the left lung. There is also a spot in the left brain. In order to know how best to treat it, we need a piece of tissue under the microscope to know exactly which type of cancer it is. The easiest area to get a piece of is the lung, that's why I spoke to the interventional radiologist. He feels he could get into the cancer with a small needle right from the outside of your chest. He could do this in the x-ray department, after numbing you up of course, and then assuming you are stable you could go home right after that. Once we get the report back, we will plan our treatment."

Lots of questions went back and forth about chemotherapy, surgery and radiation. Then Kert set up the lung biopsy and he made us an appointment with the neurosurgeon to talk about removing the tumor in Thom's head.

At the end, Kert looked at me and asked tenderly, "And how are *you* doing, Marianne?"

Those few words and that caring look on Kert's face unleashed the floodgates. I looked from Kert to Thom as I became blinded by my tears. Kert was clearly talking to me as his friend, not a colleague and not a patient's wife.

"This is all my fault," I began. "I'm the one who wanted to move back here with my whole crazy family. We built this big house that just seemed to grow and grow until it took us to near bankruptcy. The general contractors were my brother and my nephew. We loved them, but there were a lot of problems and eventually Thom had to fire them and take over the job himself. It had a terrible affect on him. He started drinking to cope. And then he just kept on drinking."

[You see, I had a theory about cancer. Our bodies make cancer cells all the time and usually our immune system detects those cells and destroys them. Why cancer cells sneak under the radar and actually form a tumor no one knows for sure, but I had long held the theory that stress had something to do with immobilizing the immune system. And if stress had caused Thom's cancer, then I was guilty.]

I paused to look at Kert, who clearly was trying to grasp what I was saying. "We worked through all that, but I know it was all that stress, all that awful stress, that allowed this cancer to happen."

Wiping my eyes as I turned to look at Thom, I apologized. "I'm so sorry, honey. I am sorry we moved here. I know you did it for me and the girls, but now I wish you hadn't. If we had moved somewhere else, this never would have happened to you."

As I sobbed into my tissues, Thom reached out and took my hand and caressed it. "Or," he began, "it could be thirty years of smoking!"

I looked up, startled. He was actually smirking at me! I almost laughed in response, but in that exact moment, I realized that he was right. It wasn't the move to Connecticut or, at any rate, if it was it only had a minor effect compared to the years he had poisoned himself with cigarettes.

I went from tears to rage in one second flat. He had done this to himself. He had done it to me. He had done it to the girls. I turned on him so fast his head must have been spinning.

"Why? Why did you do that? Why did you keep smoking?" I demanded an answer.

Kert, who I had forgotten about for the moment, jumped in. "Marianne, you did not cause your husband's cancer. And Thom certainly didn't intend to get cancer. Come on now, let's focus on how to get out of this mess and see what needs to be done next."

The tirade stopped. For now.

Thom breezed through the lung biopsy.

At the hospital, everyone was so kind and considerate, but I had the distinct impression that they were talking about us behind our backs. "That's Dr. Bette's husband and he has lung cancer, poor dear."

It was like somehow it made the staff feel worse because I was "one of them" and the patient they were treating was my husband. I never really heard anyone say those words, but their looks and actions spoke volumes.

The biopsy came back positive for an epithelial carcinoma. The fact that it had already spread told me it was an aggressive type of tumor.

Kert set Thom up for a pre-operative consult with the neurosurgeon the next day. The neurosurgeon reviewed the findings with us, answered our questions, and explained the surgery. Then he too revealed his human side by saying how much he regretted meeting us under these dire circumstances.

He had put Thom on Monday's operating schedule. His physician's assistant would come in and do a pre-op exam.

When the assistant arrived, she was shocked to see me sitting there and more distressed to find out that Thom Waner, the patient with a brain met, was my husband. You see, *she* was *my* patient…

She looked pale as she steadied herself on to the countertop in the exam room. She quickly pulled her professional self together and examined Thom. Months later when she came in to my office, we were able to talk through the awkwardness of that day.

Back at home, my mother and wife brain were in high gear. Who will watch the girls and get them off to school? What about all the other family members who don't even know Thom's going for surgery, let alone that he has cancer?

We would have to call my stepdaughter, Sarah, Thom's parents and his two brothers, Steve and John. When? Who would do that? What time was it in California, anyway? How could I change my office schedule so I could stay in the ICU with Thom?

I had this unrealistic notion that if I were by his side all the time, I could save him. At least I could calm him, and my being there would soothe him through the pain of the tubes and procedures he would have to endure.

Suddenly I heard Justine's voice. "Daddy, when they cut your head open, will it hurt?"

"No, I will be asleep. I won't even feel it." Thom paused, then he added, "You know how hard-headed I am. I probably don't have much feeling up there anyway."

Immediately the girls started to giggle. Thank God for comic relief. What a blessing a great sense of humor can be. That is when I thought about calling my cousin, Bob.

Bob was a cancer survivor. A few years back he had a nasty colon cancer. Statistically he never should have survived, but he did.

Honestly, I think he developed his survival skills by having to live through a very difficult childhood. As soon as he was able, he ran away, joined the army, and became a medic. He still tells everyone he went to Vietnam to save his life. As funny as that seems, he was dead serious.

His greatest survival skill was humor. No one looked at life like Bob. No one ever saw the fun in it that Bob did. When my mother had her colon cancer, he came to see her frequently. She looked forward to those visits more than you can imagine. He said they were in a special club, the CCC (the Colon Cancer Club). Quite the initiation!

Each time he visited, he would tell different stories about his experiences with his colon cancer and treatment. I never knew colon cancer could be so darn funny.

He told this one story about himself after his rectal surgery laying exhausted in bed the next day. This big army sergeant-type nurse came in and told him it was time to get up and get washed or she was going to do it for him. So when she went to get the towels and all, he decided to hide from her.

He got out of bed, shuffled across the room, and hid behind a curtain. But because he had no feeling in his butt and because he had a "johnny coat" on, open in the back, he didn't feel that the bed sheet was stuck in his butt crack. So despite his hiding, he left quite a tail. The story itself is funny enough, but to see him re-enact it was hilarious.

Talking to Bob would be like someone throwing me a lifeline. When I called, his immediate response was, "Okay, I understand. I'll come down tomorrow morning for a few hours." I could hold it together until he got here. Help was on its way.

Bob and his wife, Chris, sat with all of us in the kitchen while Thom filled them in on the details. It was only after all the serious conversation was done that Bob became his usual kidding self. "Hey Thom, while they are in there," he said pointing to his head, "maybe they could rearrange a few things. You know, make you a little smarter, get rid of that irritating habit you have."

The girls giggled as Thom played along. "And what irritating habit would that be?"

Bob pretended to look embarrassed. "Oh, I'm sorry. I thought you knew."

Then Bob turned to Justine and whispered, "Do you have any rubber snakes up in your room?"

Surprised, she nodded slowly.

"Well, when you go to visit your Dad in the hospital, bring a couple of those snakes with you. After your Dad has surgery, he'll have a lot of bandages around his head, like a big turban."

Justine nodded her head in agreement.

"So when the nurses aren't looking, you sneak one of those snakes out and stick it under the outer bandages with just the head sticking out."

She nodded again, smiling.

"Then just sit back and wait for the nurses to freak out. Won't that be fun?"

Finally, she laughed out loud, but Bob wasn't finished.

"And, Caitlin, how about some plastic spiders, like the kind you get around Halloween. Do you have any of those?"

When Caitlin nodded, Bob said, "Those are great to put in the bed sheets. Scares the nurses every time!"

Bob had the girls right where he wanted them. They were laughing, anticipating getting away with the perfectly executed practical joke. Only my cousin Bob could take brain surgery for cancer and turn it into an opportunity to make people laugh.

While Thom and Bob and the girls kidded around at the kitchen table, his wife, Chris, and I stood at the kitchen sink.

Quietly I asked her, "Chris, how did you deal with your feelings about Bob's cancer? I mean, he had a really nasty cancer there. Were you afraid that he wasn't going to make it?"

"I never really thought that. I just concentrated on what we needed to do to get the cure."

"Really? That was it?" She obviously did not have a doctor part of her brain talking to her.

"I don't think I could have functioned any other way."

Right then I realized that thinking about Thom *not* making it was totally paralyzing me. The arguing in my mind between the doctor, the wife and the mother was wearing me out. When my wife and mother minds were saying, "All we need right now is to be hopeful," my doctor mind was saying, "He is not going to make it."

For perhaps the first time in my life, I regretted being a doctor.

The next day, the neurosurgeon called. "Marianne, I'm canceling Thom's surgery. I've been thinking about it all weekend. I am worried that operating so close to the nerves of the arm may damage them. That would, at best, cause him to lose some function in that arm. So I have spoken to Dr. Goodrich, my colleague in New Haven. He is doing a new procedure called *gamma knife laser surgery*. It's quite possible he will give you a better outcome. At the least, you and Thom should go and talk to him and hear what he has to say."

Goodrich explained his approach. "Each person's cancer is unique. Each surgery is tailored to the individual tumor. It takes a team with a neurosurgeon, a neurophysicist and a neuroradiologist to tailor a 3D laser program to bombard each person's specific tumor. There is no traditional cutting open. There will be no incisions and no bleeding. It is all accomplished through beams of radiation outside your skull, but focused on the cancer inside your head.

"So this is what I can do for you. I think I can pinpoint that cancer within a one millimeter border of normal tissue. This is significantly smaller than traditional surgery. This should leave the nerves to the arm intact. Keep in mind that this is a new surgery. Our statistics are very promising, but there are no guarantees. You should think about it and let me know."

In typical Thom-fashion, it took him two seconds to respond. "I've thought about it. So when can we schedule it?"

Two weeks later we were at the cancer center in New Haven at 6 a.m.

Thom had to be fitted in a "halo," a two-inch wide and one half-inch thick metal circle that is held an inch from the skull like a hatband and then held in place by four metal screws. Two were screwed into the forehead and two in the back of the scalp straight through the skin and into the bone. The halo is then connected to four thick rods that are inserted into a shoulder harness that pushed his shoulders down as far as they would go.

Due to the precision of the surgery and the minute margin of error, Thom's head would be immobile in the halo and then the halo would be bolted down to the table of the linear accelerator.

To say he had to lay perfectly still was an understatement.

He was to receive 28 bolts of laser to the tumor. The laser rotated around his head as well as up and down and in and out. It looked like a bird's head with a long beak and reminded me of a woodpecker that tried from every angle to get the bugs out of tree bark. I hoped it would peck out every cancer cell.

The room looked like something out of a science fiction movie. A long thin table was in the middle of a large empty room. The table had a place for the halo to be bolted down at the far end. On the ceiling over the table was a beautiful stained glass window. I wondered how much of a distraction that offered the patients considering they had four screws in their head and were bolted down to a table. I myself would have opted for valium, but Thom said he would just meditate.

The walls outside the laser room were also decorated with beautiful stained glass images, flowers mostly. So I, too, had something lovely to look at as I paced outside the room.

It was totally silent in there. The doctors were nowhere to be seen, but I knew they would be in a protected area watching every move.

Pacing, I anticipated what would come next. *Thom will probably have a headache,* I thought, *maybe from the laser, if not, from those bolts. He will probably need to lay down in the passenger seat, maybe take some ibuprofen. I will have to be careful of how I drive, watch the potholes in the road, drive gently. I'll carefully put him to bed when we get home, and then probably pass out myself.*

When it was all over, he strutted out in his Italian loafers, wearing his jeans, a silk shirt and jacket, with his head wrapped in white gauze, like a headband. His thick black hair was sticking out of the top of the headband. I rushed over to him and asked, "Oh, honey! How do you feel?"

"I feel fine."

"You do?"

"Yep," he stated matter-of-factly.

"No headache?"

"Nope."

"You're kidding!"

"No! Actually, I'm hungry. I was thinking about going out for dinner."

"You were?" I was flabbergasted, quickly letting go of the lying-down-in-the-car scenario.

"Indian food. I saw a restaurant while we were driving around the hospital looking for a parking spot. Let's go there."

"Well, at least if we go out for Indian food, you'll fit right in with that turban on your head."

Off we went. Thom and I were laughing, silly with relief, not only of how well he came through the laser surgery, but that now he would not have to be in the ICU. He would not need to have his head cut open and a multitude of tubes in and out of his body, not to mention all the pain and emotional trauma we were now all spared. The only drawback was now there would be no spiders and snakes.

Treatment Options

*"At the end, you know what are people and what are things—
and you know where you want to put your energies."* – *Diane Bernard*

"So how does this whole brain radiation work?" I asked the radiation doctor.

Thom and I were in the basement of the hospital, where it seems that all x-ray and radiation departments are located. We sat on two wooden chairs in a small windowless room, opposite a radiation oncologist who specializes in cancerous tumors. His demeanor was what my mother would have called "mild mannered."

After looking at the x-rays and reviewing Thom's history, he talked to us about what he could do for Thom. He recommended whole brain radiation.

"Whole brain radiation gives multiple small doses of radiation to the entire brain. The idea is to catch any small new cancer cells and kill them before they can grow into a tumor."

"What about the rest of the normal cells? They get radiated too, right?"

"Normal cells are healthy and can recover. Cancer cells cannot. So, hopefully, we kill only the abnormal ones."

I didn't like the sound of that. "Hopefully?"

"Well, there will probably be some normal cells killed too."

My doctor brain needs a lot more than *hopefully, probably* and *some.* I took a deep breath, trying to figure out a diplomatic way to ask how much we were really talking about. "What do the patients and their families typically notice after the brain is radiated?"

"Typically, they lose some short-term memory." He spoke slowly, as if that would soften the blow.

My anxiety level moved up a couple of notches. How bad is this really going to be? I don't recall any of my patients having brain radiation, so this was new to me. "Like how much are we talking about here? Like they forget where they put the car keys, or they forget that they have a car?"

"Well, it differs from person to person. Some have more noticeable memory loss than others."

Alright, I think, *everyone is different and everyone has a different starting point and possibly a different ending point.* As a doctor, I also have to deal with a lot of unknowns. Each person can react differently to the same medicine at the same dose. I knew he was saying it like this because he couldn't be more specific or more accurate. He just didn't know. I got it, but I didn't like it.

But my wife brain was screaming that it needed to know something more definitive. "More radiation equals more memory loss, right?"

"Yes," he answered simply.

"So what do you think Thom will have in the way of memory loss?"

"Not much."

The brief answers to my last two questions were unsettling and disturbing to me as wife and mother. The doctor had already accepted it. I wanted enough radiation that all the cancer cells would be killed, but I wanted my husband's mind intact.

Thom, as usual, knew exactly where I was coming from. "Listen, honey," he said with a grin, "with my IQ, I could stand to lose a few brain cells. You probably won't notice a big difference."

40

I smiled, but his attempt to lighten the situation did not distract me. "Well, it's not like we have any choice either. Without the brain radiation, there is a chance of more brain tumors. I just want to know what to expect, what to look for."

Somewhere in the pit of my stomach, a gnawing overwhelming nausea was brewing. I was conjuring up the idea of what our life would be like if Thom survived all this and wound up being a 55-year-old severe dementia patient. We had always teased about being old and what it would be like if he got to be one of those "out of it" old guys with stains on the front of his shirt and pants. I used to tell him if he didn't take good care of himself, I would hire someone to come and sit with him while I went out with my friends.

Now that such an absurdity was an actual possibility, I was sick thinking about it. Thom, a mindless 55-year-old, and me holding his hand and leading him around the supermarket, buying his clothes, dressing him, wiping his mouth after he ate... Thom without a mind.

All his years of education could be wiped out by radiation. His ability to analyze and synthesize the meaning of life's experiences would all be gone. All wiped out with the whole brain eraser. Would it be quick? Like a week or two? Or would it be slow like Alzheimer's?

Visions of conversations I'd had with patients' family members flashed in rapid succession before me. I remembered their tears because their spouse or parent no longer recognized them. It was like their loved one was dead, but not really. Just their mind was.

Driving home, this weighed heavily on me. *Oh God, if this is the way it is going to be, he would be better off dead.* I knew I could deal with whatever the outcome would eventually be, but I made a mental note to myself to remember this and to know that death is not the worst possible outcome.

Am I being selfish? I thought. *I know Thom well enough to know that he too would prefer death over being brain dead. But what if I have a say here? What would I want? Could I actually vote for death?*

What about the girls? What would it be like for them taking Thom to Caitlins concert or Justines basketball games? What if he had to be led around like a child?

That awful heavy feeling in the pit of my stomach crawled up into my chest and forced all the oxygen right out of the car. Suddenly the car felt like 100°F and I started to sweat. I had to open the window for air.

I couldn't even turn to look over at Thom, who was sitting quietly next to me, probably contemplating his own demons. Could I really share all these awful thoughts with him? Would it be cruel? Was he thinking the same worst case scenario that I was?

But we had never *not* shared our deepest thoughts and fears. Not only was he my husband, but my confidante and best friend. He was the one with whom I could share my deepest hopes and fears. Now what? If I couldn't talk to him about him, who could I talk to?

We had a phrase we often used, when things got tough: We are just on for the ride. Well, this was not the ride I bargained for and I wanted off. Now.

Well, Marianne, I thought, *get over it. This is the ride you are on. Accept it. How the heck do you think Thom feels? This is not the ride he wants either!*

But he is the one who decided to smoke, I argued with myself. *He kept smoking even knowing I didn't want him to because it was dangerous.*

Well, get over it. You married him. You married a smoker. You took your chances, same as he did with you. The situation could be reversed.

Yeah, but it wouldn't be a cancer I caused myself. I wouldn't be that stupid.

The arguing in my head started to get loud—really loud. Finally, I heard three voices shout one word in unison inside my head. **Enough!**

I could feel the storm of anxiety, injustice and rage brewing. How easily I could just give into it all and go crazy. The possible negative outcomes started to incapacitate my mind and lead me toward a very dark place. I decided not to re-visit those ideas. I refused to let them overpower me.

There was no time for that now. I still had to be a wife and a mother and a doctor, all at the same time.

The Family

"It's so hard to be strong enough to let them go." – *Holly Peterson*

Justine did not understand the whole brain radiation treatments and they scared her. Knowing that children often conjure up the worst thoughts in unknown situations, Thom suggested that it might help her cope if she could see him get one of his treatments. *Always both the psychologist and the Dad*, I thought. *Why does the combination seem so effortless for him and so damn hard for me?*

Thom wore a different Hawaiian shirt each treatment, as if he were going tanning. Was that the psychologist in him, knowing the importance of a positive outlook? No, that was just Thom.

The next day we took Justine with us, Thom introduced her to everyone in the radiology department. He told her that they had made a mask to fit his face so he didn't get too sunburned. The mask was really to minimize the radiation damage to the eyes and face. Most people notice some loss in their vision after whole brain radiation, even with the mask.

"So I put the mask on," he said as he hopped onto the slick black table under the radiation beam box, "and all I have to do is lay down and they push a button, just like when you get an x-ray."

"Just like when I broke my collarbone?" she asks with surprise.

"Just like that. It doesn't even hurt. Then I'm done. The hardest part is waiting my turn."

She watched the whole process peeking over the shielded glass that the x-ray techs stand behind. I thought it might be a little unnerving for the technicians, having an 8-year-old standing there with them while they zapped her Dad's brain cancer, but they were great about the whole thing.

It was over so quickly and effortlessly that the relief in Justine's face was apparent to everyone. She skipped back out to the car. *Mission accomplished.*

It was sad, though, to see Thom hang his mask up on the x-ray room wall where it would be waiting for him tomorrow and every day after that for three weeks. Sadder still was that it was one of about eight masks there on the wall.

God bless those other masked people and their families, I thought. *They are kindred radiation spirits.*

A few days later, Justine walked home from the school bus to find Thom napping after radiation. Justine called me at the office and I could tell from her tone of voice that she was very anxious.

"Honey, what's the matter?" I asked.

"I think Dad is having another seizure."

Oh my God! My daughter is there alone with her Dad, watching him have a seizure. I quickly calculated how many minutes it would take me to get home.

But wait, I thought. *He's on anti-seizure medication, plus he already had the cancer burned out of his brain. He should not be having a seizure.*

"Why do you think that? What is he doing?"

"He's lying on the bed and he's having a hard time breathing and he's making a lot of noise."

"Like what kind of noise, Justine?"

"Listen," she said, and she put the phone close to Thom's head.

I was listening intently when I heard an obnoxious, but very familiar, sound. "It's okay, Justine. Daddy is just snoring."

"He's shaking too, Mom."

"Is he shaking all the time or just when he breathes in?" I waited a few seconds as she watched him.

"Just when he breathes in."

"That is how Daddy snores when he is very relaxed. He is in a deep sleep. He's okay, honey."

"Are you sure?"

"I am positive. He's been doing that ever since I've known him and I sleep with him every night. Believe me, sweetheart, that is not a seizure."

"Oh… Okay."

The tension was melting.

Even knowing Thom was fine, I still felt torn. Stay as the doctor with a bunch of patients waiting to be seen, or be the mother and go home to reassure my daughter that her father is only snoring?

"Are you okay now that you know Dad is only sleeping?"

"Yeah, Mom. I'm okay." she says flatly.

"I can come home if you need me."

"I'm okay. I'm going to watch a movie."

"If you are worried or have a question that is bugging you or anything, anything at all, you call me. Okay? Whenever you want." I made sure my office staff knew to come and interrupt me any time Justine called.

This was an awful lot of reality for an 8-year-old to deal with, but there was no way I could protect her from her Dad's cancer and what that meant to all of us. Justine vacillated between those stark realities and denial. I think the denial gave her the break she needed from the harshness of it all.

———————————

Since Thom was no longer able to drive due to having had a seizure, he allowed my father to drive him to radiation therapy. I am sure it wasn't just that he needed a ride. He also knew that my Dad had a sincere desire to help.

All went well for a few mornings until the day they had to take Caitlin to school first. Dad pulled up in front of the middle school and Caitlin jumped out of the back seat, then reached back in to get her backpack. This last move didn't register with my Dad though, and at that exact moment he started to pull the car away.

Caitlin stepped back from the car, but not quite fast enough. Thom saw it all.

"Joe! Stop!" Thom screamed.

Dad stopped with amazing speed for an old guy, but he stopped with the rear tire directly on top of Caitlin's foot.

"Opa, you're on my foot!" she screamed.

Caitlin was crying. Thom was yelling. And Dad was frozen in place staring at one and then the other of them. Finally, he pulled the car forward, off of Caitlin's foot.

They drove immediately to my office. Thom helped Caitlin out of the car. Through the large front office window, I saw her hopping on one foot with tears streaming down her face.

Thom was both pale and at a loss for words, as if in mid-asthma attack. After getting Caitlin into my office, he immediately laid down on the couch panting. While I examined Caitlin's foot, Thom related the story to me through clenched teeth.

Her toes were bruised, but warm. The foot was swollen, but all bones moved well with an amount of pain that let me know they weren't broken. We iced her foot and Thom started to regain his color and breathe more evenly.

My father, on the other hand, was pacing back and forth in the waiting room, wringing his black beret in his hands. He almost sprung to my side as I opened door.

"Is she alright?" he pleaded as soon as I opened the door.

"Yes, Dad. She's alright. Nothing is broken."

"Oh thank God," he sighed in relief. Then he started grabbing for words to explain the inexplicable. "I don't know what happened, Marianne. I thought she was out of the car. I didn't know…"

"It's okay, Dad," I said, taking his hand. "She is going to be fine." He was now the third patient to care for in the car-on-foot incident.

He refused to come back to where Caitlin was, despite my repeatedly reassuring him that there would be no long-term damage. He was eventually able to calm down enough to take Thom to his radiation therapy, while Caitlin stayed with me.

It reminded me of what I knew to be true with my patients, that when someone in the family is seriously ill, the whole family is ill. My father could not concentrate both on getting his cancerous son-in-law to his radiation treatments and take his granddaughter to school.

That was the last time Dad drove Thom to radiation. In fact, it was the last time he drove anyone in our family anywhere. It was just too stressful.

During the second week of whole brain radiation, Thom woke up one morning and there was an awful lot of hair on the pillow.

"Hey, look at that," he said, pointing to his furry pillow.

"Looks like you are shedding," I replied.

After repeating the performance for the next three days, he looked like he had a moth-eaten scalp.

"Can you help me shave my head?" he asked on the fourth day.

"Don't you want to go to the barber and just have it trimmed really short?"

"Nope. It's going to look pretty bad, so let's just shave it off."

Shaving Thom's head was one of the weirdest feelings I had ever experienced. I was concentrating very carefully so that I wouldn't cut his scalp, and then he'd not only have no hair, but also a nice bunch of red scabs on his bald head.

It was completely different from shaving my own legs. First of all, I had no sense of how much pressure to exert since I didn't have the tactile feedback. But also, his head was round. I'd never shaved round before. So it took me two or three times around to get all the hair off.

When I finished, I stood there watching him looking at himself in our huge bathroom mirror. His scalp was glistening white. It was one of those very quiet, very momentous moments.

There are times, and especially dramatic times like this, when so much can fly through your brain that you can hardly take stock of it all.

I was looking at my husband, bald. For the 16 years I had known him, he had the most gorgeous head of thick wavy black hair. Not even a receding hair line. Now he had none.

How perfect his head was! Who knew? With that shiny white scalp, his black eyebrows seemed so prominent and his eyes so brown. Looking at him as he looked at himself, I wondered how he must be feeling about this tremendous change in himself.

"What do you think?" I asked cautiously.

"Well, I think I'll need a ride."

"A ride? Where to?"

"Looks like I'll have to join the skinheads now. Any idea where they congregate?"

How does he do it? Just when I feel my emotions careening out of control, he cracks me up. Laughing and crying offer the same release, but I definitely prefer laughing.

I hugged his bald head and kissed it. What an odd feeling, lips on bare smooth scalp. Oh well, just another superficial thing to let go of. No big deal. I mean, really. It's just hair.

———————————— ✦ ————————————

There were some odd side effects from Thom's brain surgery and radiation. He had always had a loud voice and a quick response in conversation, but after the surgery, he slowed down and spoke more softly. He occasionally had difficulty finding the exact words he wanted.

Sometimes he would choose a word very close to the word he wanted and then he would correct himself. "No, that's not what I wanted to say. What I wanted to say is _____," then the right word would come.

When the right word wouldn't come, he'd say the definition of the word he wanted and then look at you, waiting for you to supply the right one.

All this had the most unexpected effect on the person with whom he was in conversation. They would be very drawn in, almost leaning forward on their seat to participate in helping him communicate.

Once I commented to him about it. He said that his speech center must have been slightly damaged by the gamma knife. He had deliberately slowed down his speech to allow it to catch up with his thinking. He too had noticed how engaging that process was for his listeners. If he had only known this earlier in his career, he said, he would have been able to use it as a technique to communicate more effectively with his patients.

We discovered another odd side effect one night while Thom was washing the dishes. I was clearing the last of the dishes from the table and stacking the dishwasher. Thom was washing the pots and pans in the sink.

"Oh, honey, here is one more thing," I said, bringing over a big glass platter that had been a wedding gift of ours.

"Okay. Put it there." He pointed to the counter next to the sink. We kept talking as I wiped down the kitchen table. Suddenly, I heard a huge crash and the sound of glass breaking in the sink.

"Are you alright?" I asked, rushing over to him.

He was looking into the sink as if there was an apparition floating around in the water. "I picked it up and it just slipped out of my hand as if I wasn't even holding it! I didn't even feel it let go!" He looked at his left hand covered in soapy water as if it were not even his own.

"Was it in your left hand?" I asked.

"Yes."

"Well that's where they zapped the brain tumor. It probably knocked out a few of your sensory nerves as well." He continued to look stunned and dejected as he rinsed off his hands.

"Anyway, I am glad you broke that platter." I added.

"Really?"

"Oh yeah," I said as I put the biggest broken pieces in a thick brown paper trash bag. "The truth is, I never really liked that platter, but since it was a wedding present I felt obligated to keep it. Now I get to throw it out."

"Well, I'm glad to be so helpful," he giggled with relief.

Even if that platter had been one of my favorites, I would have said it wasn't. Once your spouse is battling cancer, there is no earthly possession worth more than trying to make him feel better about his own body and what he is going through.

After we cleaned up the broken glass, he was wiping down the sink and I came up and hugged him from behind.

"Just because you're breaking things, don't think this will get you out of washing the dishes," I teased. I could feel his muscles relax as I held him.

"Do me one favor, though, will you?" I whispered into his ear. "Keep away from the Waterford crystal."

Sarah's Story

"If we know anything, we know there is a beginning and an end. Yet we avoid the end and how to live up to that point." – Deb Bette

Even though Thom's daughter, Sarah, didn't live with us, she was a significant part of our life.

Since I had known the two of them there always seemed to be something wanting in their relationship. It might have been about timing. Times when he wanted her to live with us and she did too, but her Mom didn't. Times when she didn't want him (or me), but we wanted her. Somehow, the timing just never seemed right for everyone, until now.

This time, it was clear. He wanted her to come and she wanted to be here with him more than anything.

When we were dating, Thom couldn't wait to show off Sarah to me. He acted like she was his most prized possession (because in a way she was).

All three of us were excited to be meeting each other.

She was an animated 8-year-old who couldn't sit still in the back seat of the car. Her light brown pony tail on the top of her head was pulled over to one side and bounced around, punctuating every sentence. Her pink star earrings dangled and sparkled along with her eyes.

She laughed and chewed gum in equal profusion between firing off a hundred questions at me. Did I like her Dad's cooking? How long had I been a doctor? Could she see my house? Could she spend the night? Did I know her Mom had a boyfriend? Now her Dad had a girlfriend. They each had someone and that made her happy.

On our first meeting, we planned to spend the day at an amusement park in Los Angeles. The three of us were deliriously happy. Being together was more fun than any of the rides. My cheeks ached from all the smiling and laughing. I was smitten with Sarah from that day on.

We had Sarah every other weekend, as is so typical of divorced parents. We were a pretty happy threesome. Before bed, I read to her from *The Secret Garden*, and snuggled her as she fell asleep. Always looking forward to our time together, I was determined to be the best stepmother I could be.

Sarah's mother and I could not have been more different. Her mother lived in a house on Santa Monica beach, right next to the infamous "Muscle Beach." She was a psychic channeler. She channeled spirits' thoughts "from the other side." I lived on the top of a mountain overlooking the Mojave Desert and I was a family doctor. Enough said.

Could Sarah take the best from the two very different lifestyles in which she lived? I hoped so.

One day Sarah and I were driving down the freeway. After a few minutes of quiet she said, "It's hard to believe a dead person can talk through my mother's mouth."

Feeling like I was just rear-ended, I quickly tried to collect my thoughts. I had some definite opinions about her mother's style of child-raising, which I had only shared with Thom. I felt Sarah's mother had abdicated her parental responsibilities too often to "the spirits."

At that moment, I was tempted to unleash my true feelings. My temperature rose and my ears prickled with the heat of an angry stepmother. Part of me wanted to validate her feelings and tell her that her mother was nuts. It was just the two of us, and she was revealing some doubt about her mother. At that moment, I could have said anything.

My mind raced through several scenarios. Sarah spent most of her time with this woman. She loved her mother and her mother loved her. Although it wasn't a brand of mothering I could relate to, it was still a loving relationship. What was to be gained on Sarah's part for my discrediting her mother in her eyes?

"Yup," I said slowly, "it sure is."

Sarah's face fell a little bit. When I saw that, I added, "but who knows. There really is no way to test it. So no one knows for sure." That is how I knew I was in love with Sarah. I was willing to let go of my agenda, because hers was more important.

———————————— ✦ ————————————

I didn't become the "evil stepmother" until Sarah turned 13. That was when our every-other-weekend visits ended.

It must have been difficult for her to go from her beach home to her desert home and all that the transition entailed. Maybe she got tired of the contrasts or maybe she just chose the path of greater personal freedom.

Either way, the visits over the next two years could have been counted on two hands. Those decisions were made between her parents and her. Whatever I said meant nothing to her mother, and I had no bearing on what Sarah did at her mother's house.

Complaining to Thom just put him in a position of conflict. He too had little to no effect on Sarah's mother. What actually went on with Sarah and her mother, and how she was parented, I don't know. For everyone's sanity, I gave up trying to understand, much less have any input.

One night a few years later, there was a lot of animated talking going on the phone with Thom to Sarah and her mother. I was paying bills at the kitchen table and only heard occasional snatches of their conversation.

When it was over, Thom walked over to me and as he came closer I saw an odd look on his face. It looked as if he had just pulled his fingers out of an electric socket. His black hair seemed to be standing straight up, his breathing was ragged, and he was pale with anger.

"Sarah's pregnant."

"What?" I exploded.

"Yup, and she is five month's along."

"You have got to be kidding," I responded stunned.

"No. She and her mother colluded to keep it from us so we wouldn't put any pressure on her to terminate the pregnancy."

"Well there is no chance of that now, not at five months. Why the heck did her Mom do that?" I was incredulous.

"Pam said Sarah always wanted to have a baby." He sounded like he was reciting a line from some bad play.

What woman in this day and age would actually think that her 15-year-old daughter having a baby was a good idea? That fact completely blew my mind and terminally changed my opinion of her mother. I was sorry I ever supported her. She was mentally challenged in some way that defied definition.

"What the heck did you ever see in that nut case?" I hurled at Thom.

"I don't know, but that's why I divorced her."

We looked at each other as if a bomb just went off. Nothing in our faces, our room, our lives or our minds felt familiar. It seemed as if we were on some mind-altering drug having a bad trip. Now what should we do? What *can* we do?

"Okay, so who is the father?" I asked. Maybe there would be someone on that side of the situation we could relate to. Maybe the baby's father would be able to lend a shred of common sense to this nightmarish situation. Maybe his parents would be a help.

"Some gangbanger from East LA." A teenage gang member.

"Oh, for God's sake, this story gets more unbelievable every minute. If it was on TV, you would think the script writers got carried away."

"Yeah, and Pam is still planning on moving to Montana."

"Is Sarah going too?"

"No."

"No? Sarah's pregnant, and she is going to abandon her too?" I was beginning to gain some insight into what motivated people into manslaughter, or in this case woman-slaughter.

I wanted this woman to pay for allowing this kid not only to get pregnant, but to encourage her to think that having a baby as a 15-year-old child is a good idea. Most 20-year-olds don't even know what they are getting into when they plan to have a child.

Let's get real here. Sarah was a child having a child.

"Is she coming to live with us?" Living with an acting out pregnant teenager was not really what I wanted, but I would do it for Sarah.

"No," he stated flatly.

Now I wasn't sure if I was relieved or even more worried.

"No? So where is she going to live?"

"She is going to live with the boyfriend and his family in East LA." (The Mexican slums of LA.)

"In the barrio?!" I yelled in disbelief.

"You got it."

"Holy shit!" By now I was pacing and looking at the floor as if somewhere there I could find a clue telling me this was all some kind of ridiculous hoax.

I looked at Thom and saw he was in a similar state of mind-numbing shock, looking down but not seeing the floor, rather seeing the evaporating childhood of his 15-year-old daughter.

"All this has been going on in these last few months since we haven't seen Sarah." I said this more to myself, like somehow if I said it out loud it might make more sense to me.

"You are *not* going to let her go live in the barrio are you?"

"Well, I'm going to call up that boy's father and go down to dinner and assess the family and the situation for myself." He said, obviously just thinking it through.

"Wait a minute… You are inviting yourself to dinner at their house?" I asked in disbelief.

"Yup." He said it as if he thought it was a good idea.

Both of us were bent over opposite sides of the kitchen island, each of us with one hand to our temples and the other grasping the counter top as if that could ground us in some emotional or physical way. The emotional hurricane blew our minds, leaving us stripped and raw.

"Yes, I am going to go down there and check out the boy and his family."

He was talking matter-of-factly now, calmly. He seemed inappropriately in control. Would he go down there and blow up? Or would he be lost in the barrio with the gangs, beaten up or worse?

"You are not going down there angry or to start a fight are you?" I queried peering into his eyes.

"Marianne," he said in a more calm way than I would have imagined possible. "Sarah is already 5 months pregnant. She stopped her birth control pills on purpose. She *chose* this boy. She wants to be with him. There is no changing that. I honestly want to see what kind of people they are, and to make sure that my daughter will be safe. If she is going to live with them, I am paying them room and board so she is not obligated to them."

Put in that framework, it made sense. Despite the unreality of the situation, it made total sense, and I too could see that it was the best plan. How could he put things like that together so quickly? Maybe all those years of being a psychotherapist had taught him to be sharp like that.

No matter how he was able to do it, I was in awe of his flexibility and his insight, especially considering it was his own daughter. It took a lot of manly courage to both conceive and execute that plan, but he did it. That feat had me completely revamp my idea or definition of a "real man." Anyone who could and would do that deserved my highest esteem.

Thom actually liked the parents. They were two hard-working Mexican immigrants who were also surprised and disappointed by the behavior of these two teenagers. All the adults wanted an easier life for these two than the life they chose for themselves.

The details were worked out and Sarah moved in with Mario and his family. Sarah went to alternate education classes with several of her pregnant Chicana girlfriends. A few brought their infants with them. We actually saw more of Sarah those last four months of her pregnancy than we had for the preceding two years. Initially, she brought her boyfriend, Mario, with her to our house. The last few months of her pregnancy, however, he was in the juvenile detention area of our local prison for some gang-related violence. (I doubt I'll ever know the true story behind that.)

She would often walk the hills around our house, looking longingly toward the prison miles away to where Mario was incarcerated. One time, we were not far from the prison and I drove around it to check it out. All that chain-link fencing with shiny steel barbed-wire curlicues around the top made the hair on my arms stand straight up.

Sarah thought it was great to be "so close to Mario." It's no wonder I lost weight during that time.

Watching Thom handle that entire situation with Sarah taught me a lot. Handling disappointments and frustrations with your own children can tax you to your limit and beyond. Somehow you have to push the limits out farther.

And there are different limits for different kids. As we would say at those frustrating times, "It's only a baby. It's not AIDS, it's not drugs, and it's not alcohol." Now of course we'd add, "It's not cancer."

If it's not something life-threatening, you will survive. It's a situation you can live with or learn from, or both. You literally have to, so why not adopt a positive attitude?

A week or so after Mario III was born, Sarah turned 16. She took Driver's Ed, continued on in school and maintained her exceptional grades.

Despite her age, she was a great mother and it was clear she was trying her best. One day, when Thom and I were talking about how well she was handling her life, we thought about what we could do to help her.

He said, "I want to buy her a car."

At first, I thought it was crazy, but the more I thought about it, the more I liked the idea. Now she would have a "getaway" vehicle. Hopefully, the day would come when Sarah would wake up and realize that she and her baby did not belong in the barrio.

Whenever that was, I wanted her to have the freedom to just get in her own car and leave. A car was crucial to the getaway-dream scenario.

At times when I thought I would go crazy with worry for her and "little Mario," I prayed for the getaway day to come. I visualized her getting in her car and having the will and the freedom to leave. When she finished Driver's Ed, we bought her a new Toyota Corolla. The rise in her self-esteem was almost palpable. Seeing her driving around in it did us a world of good. Seeing her act like any happy 16-year-old driving her new car with a huge grin on her face, Thom and I felt as if she didn't lose every common teenage experience, even if she did have her son in the car seat beside her.

Almost one year later, Sarah showed up at our house with baby Mario and her car packed to the brim. She had left the boyfriend and East LA for good. She was headed out to high school in Montana and to live with her mother.

During that brief goodbye visit, she made me cry. She told me how she understood now what I was trying to do for her back then when I was parenting her in ways she thought were so restrictive. She realized that I mothered her the way I did because I truly loved her and wanted the best for her. She said that, in some ways, I was her mentor for mothering. I felt exonerated and relieved. Some deep dammed up place where all stepparents push their frustration and anger just let go. Then we were both bawling like babies with a new appreciation and love for each other. I felt like throwing a party, like when the prodigal son returns home.

Within three months of being in Montana, she was in the National Honor Society, playing soccer on her high school team and making plans to go to her junior prom. (Her Mom had promised to babysit little Mario.)

After three years in Montana, Sarah transferred to a college in Santa Barbara, California. She worked part-time to support her son, Mario, and herself, and she went to school part-time as well. It was a lot to take on for a 23-year-old single Mom, but she did it well.

She was in the Drama department and enjoying school. In fact, she was awarded a scholarship from the university to take a one-month workshop in England for directing and acting.

She would be flying to England around August, right over us. She wasn't planning to stop and see her Dad. Thom had somehow conveyed to everyone in his family that his lung cancer was like a cold!

"Yeah," I heard him say once, "I've got garden-variety lung cancer. I'll have to take chemotherapy for six months to get rid of it."

I was absolutely floored. As a doctor I was thinking, *Where did he get that ridiculous idea?* Besides, who in their right mind would ever use "garden variety" in the same sentence with cancer? I knew he was trying to allay any fears that his family in California would have, but would Sarah listen to her Dad's analysis of his health and pass up an opportunity to spend time with him while he was feeling relatively well?

I started to feel like a doomsayer, but Sarah had to have a more realistic understanding.

"Sarah? It's Marianne," I whispered.

"Marianne? I can hardly hear you. Where are you?"

"I'm in my closet."

"Your closet? But why—?"

"Sarah, I am calling to tell you that you should come out and see your Dad on one leg of your trip to or from London."

"Really?" she asked, obviously surprised.

"Listen, I know your Dad is acting like his cancer cure is a done deal. But I have to tell you, my doctor brain says there is a chance that he is not going to beat this. Look, it's cancer. No one can predict how it will respond or what the outcome is going to be. I don't know exactly what your Dad's chances are, but there is a definite chance he may not beat it."

"Really? I didn't know that."

"I know. That is why I am calling, you need to know that although the tumor in his lung is small, the fact that it was already in his head when we found it is a bad sign. Most importantly, if he doesn't beat this cancer and you had passed up a chance to spend time with him when he was in fairly good health, I think you might really regret it later."

Silence.

"You know what I mean?" I nudged.

"Yeah," she answered slowly. I could almost hear the wheels turning in her mind, even across the country. Then she added huskily, "I sure would."

"See if you can work it out. We could pick you up at the airport."

"Thanks. I'll see what I can do and get back to you."

"Oh, and Sarah?"

"Yes?"

"Your Dad does *not* know I am having this conversation with you."

"I figured that, Marianne. You don't usually make calls from your closet."

Sarah came and spent five wonderful days with her Dad.

They were both hopeful for a positive outcome, and didn't let Thom's cancer keep them from enjoying the time together.

Living With Cancer

"Cancer is a gift of time—the time in which to say your goodbyes."
— Caitlin Bette-Waner

After completing the three weeks of whole brain radiation, Thom started chemotherapy. Since he took a large dose through a tube directly into his vein, he only had to go to the office every two or three weeks.

It's hard to believe, but a person settles into a routine with chemotherapy. You actually calm down at this point. The shock of diagnosis is over. The second opinions are collected. The Tumor Board has reviewed your case, and you and your oncologist have planned the most appropriate chemotherapy program. Now you just have to take it and see if it works.

Your life still goes on—you shop, you eat, you sleep, you visit with friends. You are still alive. You are tired, but alive, and grateful for that.

Thom could no longer work in my office, nor be exposed to people who were sick. As chemo kills the cancer cells, it also kills the healthy white blood cells (the ones you need to fight off infection) as well as healthy red blood cells. So your red blood cell count gets low. (It's called "anemia.")

Most significantly, you get very tired. You wake up tired, your energy stays low all day, and no amount of espressos or naps help. You go to bed exhausted, just like you began the day.

As we progressed into the fall, Thom became tremendously intolerant to the cold. Our whole marriage, I was the one who was always cold. I wanted the heat turned up and more blankets on, and I could feel the draft from outside when the door was open before anyone else. Now, thanks to chemo, Thom was the one who was always cold.

One night, as we so often did, we were sitting in the great room in front of a blazing fire.

Our great room was a large open cathedral-ceilinged space that was off of our dining room. The fireplace took up one end. At the opposite end was a grand piano. Between the two were two velvet–covered couches facing one another (a plum-colored one and a green one) with a low oak table in between that was ideal for putting my feet up on at the end of the day.

Even though it was the largest room in the house, the eclectic furnishings and close proximity to each other lent the room a cozy feel.

Reclining on the purple couch under a down throw, I was lost in the flames licking over the logs as the fire snapped and crackled. Thom was in his usual position facing the fire as he rocked in my great-grandmother's oak platform rocker. It was his favorite chair, and was on the opposite side of the oak table from the fireplace. After my mother gave it to us, he had it recovered in a garnet-colored velvet—the little head rest, the back, the seat and the padded arms.

Despite its springs' many oilings, we were never able to get rid of the little creaking noise it made when it rocked forward. The rhythmic creaking of the old chair rocking and the fire had lulled us both into a peaceful reverie.

It's funny how I didn't even notice the rocking chair noise until it stopped. Without thinking about it, I turned toward the rocker and Thom. He was consumed with shivering and shaking from head to toe.

"Honey!" I said. "What's wrong?"

"I'm cold," he chattered.

"I see that." I threw my down blanket over him. It had no effect. *Get him warm. He has the teeth-chattering chills.* I heard inside my head.

Having had good wilderness first aid training, I knew that the best way to warm up a cold or wet body is to strip the person down and put them in a sleeping bag with another stripped-down warm body.

Hustling him in to the bedroom, I threw the extra blankets on the bed. Thom stood there with the soft down blanket clutched over his shoulders. He was shaking so bad he almost couldn't keep his balance.

"You have to get your jeans off, Thom," I said.

"Help me," he chattered.

I struggled to pull the jeans down his shivering body. He was not helping at all. *Where is he?* It was as if he was popcorn popping around next to the bed.

Pulling the shirt over his head made him loose his balance. His arms flew out like an acrobat on a tight rope. I steadied him and placed his hands on the footboard of the bed. "Hold on to the bed."

Even though he may have thought I was crazy pulling off his clothes to get him warm, he didn't resist my directions.

Tucking him under all the covers, I quickly stripped off my clothes and dove into bed next to him. I wrapped my body on and around him, a human blanket. Pulling the covers over our heads my only thought was *heat.*

Three minutes later, the major shakes stopped and shortly after that he was warm.

What a relief I felt when his body stop shaking under mine! He warmed up and felt like his muscles were melting under my weight. Then he passed out.

When I asked Kert what that was all about, I found out this was a common occurrence in cancer patients. It's called the "chemotherapy shakes."

In fact, some of my cancer patients spoke about it to me later on. I sure wish I had known before it happened to Thom. What good was all my medical training and experience if I didn't know simple things like the chemo shakes?

Seeing him so overwhelmed by his own out-of-control body was a shock to the wife in me. When had he become so vulnerable? Why did I think he wouldn't be? I needed to ramp up my awareness. My husband had no choice but to take whatever came his way. I vowed to stay more on top of his physical needs and try to anticipate and prepare for them. How I was going to do this I had no idea, but it didn't stop me from making the commitment.

The next day I went to Macy's and bought a king-sized red electric blanket with dual controls. Each afternoon when I came home I turned it on as a preventative measure so we would never have to repeat the brutal performance of the previous day. The blanket had a pre-heat setting, just like an oven. It would get as hot as it could in the shortest time possible.

Thom found that he could lay his pajamas on top of the blanket and while the bottom was heating the bed, the top also heated his PJs. Apparently his adaptive mechanisms were not completely compromised. While we continued our nights in front of the fire, there was the electric blanket waiting on high.

That was not the only night we were totally incapacitated by the shakes. The next time, I was prepared for what would happen to Thom, but not to the rest of us.

It makes sense that any mother with a distraught or grieving child would most likely be in the same distraught or grieving mental state herself.

Stress was a way of life now at our house. Sometimes my maternal instincts were nowhere to be found. Thankfully, Justine had always been a verbal child. If I wasn't paying attention to her and she was needy or feeling strongly about something, she would let me know. Most often, it was in an obnoxious way that got my attention—Justine's "zingers" I would call them.

One night after dinner, Justine decided that she wanted to have "special family time" in the great room. While Caitlin, Thom and I cleaned up the kitchen, she was in the great room lighting candles and setting the mood for the four of us.

Right then, Thom got one of his chemo shakes. I rushed him into the bedroom and under the waiting heated blanket. It still took a few minutes for him to get warmed up. Justine was impatiently sitting on the purple couch in the great room waiting for Thom to come out. But those attacks were not only exhausting, they were debilitating.

Once Thom got warm, he was almost unable to move. The thought of getting out of that warm bed and going into the living room was more than Thom could handle. Caitlin assessed the situation and quickly adapted as she hopped right into bed and snuggled with her Dad. Not so with Justine, she was holding out for the family to return to her "romantic" living room scenario. One look at Thom told me he was not moving, even to please his daughter and I wasn't going to let him.

"I'm sorry, Justine. Daddy is not going to be able to come back into the great room," I informed her. She was sitting there in the candlelight by herself, waiting.

"But I want him to," she answered emphatically.

"I know you do, honey, but he can't come out. He's too tired. Why don't you come into the bedroom?"

"No, I don't want to come in there. I want him to come out here."

How quickly the battle lines were drawn. She was heavily invested in her idea of what the night would be and was not going to let go of it. The wife in me was protecting her husband, while the mother was looking at a willful, obstinate child who wanted her own way no matter what. That was *not* going to happen.

I said she could come to our room or go to hers—those were her options. She refused. Eventually I got angry and lost control and literally hauled her upstairs to her bedroom. She was screaming and wailing. I told her to stay there until she could be better behaved. Then she could come down and join us.

Justine's bedroom is directly over our bedroom, and we could hear her screaming and crying until she actually had herself hysterical. She came downstairs and was at our bedroom door, crying, pale and gasping for air. I asked her if she wanted to come in and she defiantly said "No!"

I was so mad that there was no empathy left in my body. Zero. I made her go back upstairs to her room.

The three of us tried to maintain our family cohesiveness in the room below an 8-year-old in full-blown tantrum. I noticed she was now not only hysterical, but getting worse by the minute. I intended to ride it out and let her slow down, but it was clear that was not going to happen. Then the mother light went on in my head.

What the heck are you doing, Marianne? She's a kid. She had her plans for a special evening ruined by something totally out of anyone's control. She wanted to spend some special time with her Dad, who has cancer, and with the rest of her family. She did her best to set the mood for an intimate gathering. How much more important does it get? Now you have excluded your youngest child from the ones she wanted to entertain. While the three of you are snuggling in another room, she is upstairs, hysterical. Marianne get back up there. Now!

Boy! I felt like a bad mother.

I knocked on her door. "Go away," she hissed between sobs.

When I insisted on coming in, she dove under the bed.

"Stay away!" she said emphatically.

"Come on out, honey."

"No! I hate you."

"I know you are mad at me."

"You are mean."

"I'm sorry. I didn't realize how important this was to you."

"That's because all you pay attention to is Dad. You don't even notice me."

In her eyes, that was true. I laid down on the floor beside her bed. "Well it's true that I pay a lot of attention to Dad these days, but that's because he is so needy right now. It doesn't mean that you don't count or that you're not important too."

I was thinking fast, praying to find some way to reach my daughter, to communicate to this hurting child that there has to be a balance between her needs and her Dad's. But at this exact minute, her need was greater.

She remained firmly ensconced under the bed. I tried to get a little closer to her.

"Don't come under here or I'll poke you," she warned, grabbing her back scratcher and aiming it at me.

"I don't blame you for being mad." I waited. She was listening. "I know how important it is not to be left out, especially for you. There the rest of us were in our bedroom and I made you come up here by yourself. That was the wrong thing to do, Justine. I am sorry. I wasn't seeing it from your point of view."

"That's for sure."

"I guess I'm not thinking very well either," I admitted. Now I started talking more slowly and even-tempered. "Sometimes the stress gets to me too. I have never gone through this before. It's all new to me, and I'm making mistakes—like I did tonight with you. But it's not that you are not important to me. Please don't ever think that. You are so important to me."

"Yeah?"

I could hear the hope in her voice. "Actually, as hard as it may be for you to believe it right now, I couldn't live through this without you, Justine."

"You couldn't?"

"No way. You are so important and precious to me, but I can see that I need to let you know that. And I need to let you know that more often. I need to pay more attention to how you are doing."

Silence.

"Well, I'm planning on doing that." I paused, waiting. "Could you come out here now?"

"No."

I really wanted to be closer to her. "Could I come under there?"

"Okay," she agreed.

I tried to squeeze along the oak floor under the bed slats, but I was prevented by a strong wave of claustrophobic nausea and panic. I involuntarily scooted right out. "I'm sorry. I can't stay under there, Justine. It's too scary for me. Could I just hold your hand?"

"Why is it too scary?" she asked.

I decided to tell her my story. Maybe then she would be able to see me as a person with her own vulnerabilities.

"When I was little, about your age, I was playing hide-and-seek with my younger brother, Pete—your Uncle Pete. We were playing while my parents were having a party in the living room. I ran to the far end of the house and hopped into my parents' hope chest at the foot of their bed. When Pete finally came to the last room to look for me, I scrunched all the way down in the hope chest so he couldn't see me.

"The top closed and locked. I didn't know it until he was gone. When I tried to sit back up and open the lid, it wouldn't open. I tried to force it, hitting the inside with my back. I bucked like crazy to force the lid open, but it was jammed tight. I just kept trying until I honestly thought I was going to die from suffocation and the smell of moth balls.

"I don't know how long he was gone, nor do I know how long it took for my parents to notice that they hadn't seen me for awhile. But it felt like I was locked in that hope chest for a lifetime. I honestly thought I would die in there.

"Later, when I heard my parents screaming for me, I started bucking against the lid again. By the time my parents found me, the lid was jammed and my Dad had to break it open to get me out. I flew out like a jack-in-the-box.

"I remember my Dad trying to hold me. He was having a hard time because my arms and legs kept flying out from my body uncontrollably while I gasped and screamed. He had to hold me tight for a very long time, because each time he let me go I would start in again. He kept petting my head and my hair telling me I was alright now. I remember wanting to believe it, but not being able to. It took a really long time for me to calm down.

"Ever since that day, I have a hard time when I get in tight spaces, like under your bed. I get the feeling that I won't be able to breathe. Just like when I was in that hope chest."

As Justine took in the story, she reached out to hold my hand. I could feel her anger turning to empathy. I wanted her to see her mother's human side. I wanted her to know that I can make mistakes too. But most of all, I wanted her to feel her mother's love. We held hands silently for a few minutes.

Still holding my hand, she started to come out from under the bed. She came close enough for me to pull her slowly into an embrace. We held each other. We took a deep breath and exhaled in unison.

"Maybe we could have a pact? You and me?" I suggested.

"What's that?" she asked.

"It's a solemn promise between two people," I explained.

"I promise to pay more attention to you. You promise to be more cooperative."

I hugged and kissed her, and she let me. After a minute she said, "I can try, Mom. but I'm not promising for sure. I'm stressed too."

Caitlin's assimilation of Thom's cancer was so quiet that it almost went unnoticed.

"Can I do anything for you, Daddy?" she would ask softly.

More often than not Thom's response was, "Yes, honey. Leave the door open to my bedroom, go into the great room and play the piano for me."

Caitlin has played a musical instrument ever since kindergarten. (Thankfully, we endured only one painful year of violin.) She had been playing the piano for several years by this time. She practiced daily and her progress was obvious.

Unlike Justine, to understand Caitlin I had to consciously observe her at a slight distance to know her mood. On quiet afternoons, she would be slowly walking around in the great room.

Was she thinking about what she might play? Was the piano "calling" to her?

The red mahogany finish we chose was to match the wood trim in the great room. But once it was home, all I could see was how well the piano matched the red highlights in my daughter's hair.

Sitting on the piano bench she would compose herself with a few slow deep breathes. Slightly arched small porcelain fingers poised on the ivory keys. Eyes closed and head bent, their communication continued. Soon she and the piano were in some intimate conversation whose goal was to quiet the mind while her fingers danced effortlessly over the keys.

Caitlin often played whatever piece she was working on, but Thom's most frequent request was Pachelbel's Canon.

Initially, she played to soothe her Dad. But somewhere along the route she traveled with him, ultimately arriving at his destination with him almost as if she carried him on her fingertips, they arrived at a place where there was no pain, only support and transcendence. Transported together, one leading, the other following—parent and child, teacher and taught, healer and healed—two souls suspended in the clouds above the world and its reality.

While she played there was only weightlessness, togetherness and living completely in the moment, totally transfixed to the here and now.

I could hear it, I could see it and I could feel it. Occasionally I could even ride on their coattails.

After she played, I often found Caitlin silently enveloped in her Dad's arms. There was a warm vibration emanating from them that was like two swimmers collapsed together in post-race exhaustion.

When she wasn't playing the piano, she found other ways to reach her father. The kitchen table was often covered in construction paper, scissors, glue, glitter sequins and colored felt-tip pens. From these she would create homemade cards with encouraging thoughts or phrases.

Dragonflies were often included since they were Thom's favorites. Dragonflies symbolize the soul in Native American spirituality. Once she found these adorable blue and green iridescent dragonflies with little suction cups on them, and she stuck them on our bathroom mirror so Thom could see them every day. They are still there to this day.

So many little things she did in the well-wishing and later in the goodbying. So thoughtful. So Caitlin.

Of course, Caitlin had her human side too. As well as she handled herself, there were times when her stress showed through like the rest of us. She was more argumentative then.

One time, Thom reprimanded her for losing her special graphing calculator. Again. It was somewhere in school. This was just another thing in a long list of items she had lost, including her glasses, textbooks, homework assignments, and various shoes and clothing.

She bridled under the rebuke. "Well, you don't have a chance to lose anything," she hurled back at her Dad, "because you don't go anywhere. All you do is sit at home and do nothing!"

The wife in me responded in knee-jerk fashion. "Caitlin! Dad has the hardest job of us all. He has to fight cancer all day long. He has to fight nausea. He has to fight depression too. It may not look like he is doing much to you, but believe me he is in full battle mode. He is fighting as if his life depends on it, because it does."

Hurt often comes out as anger. Caitlin was angry about Thom's withdrawal from her and from our everyday life. Surely each child perceives it the very day it happens, but there is often a delayed reaction. Initially, she did not let it bother her, but after enough days piled up when her Dad wasn't there, she got angry. She was able to contain it until she was really hurt and needy. Then she wanted to hurt back. That's just human nature.

Every child has an instinctive knack for knowing exactly where their parents' weak spots are, as well as the opportune time to attack them.

In her first year of a new and challenging high school, Caitlin was taxed to her limit. Dealing with her Dad's declining physical health, not to mention a mother who came unglued on her occasionally, was more than she could handle at times. She would then retreat into schoolwork or music or her friends.

"I wish I could lay around the house all day like you, Dad" popped out of her one day.

It was an innocent statement, really. There was no meanness or nastiness in it. She was exhausted and every time she saw her Dad, he was doing what she wanted to do for herself: rest. Thom looked at her as if she was speaking a foreign language. I saw him blanch and immediately sprang to Thom's defense.

"Oh sure, Caitlin," I said in a snotty voice. "All you have to do is get cancer, take chemo until you puke, and feel like crap 24/7. Then you'll see how great it feels to 'lay around all day.'"

What a mean mother I was becoming. I verbally attacked my own daughter. Holy crap! I became more and more protective of Thom in almost every way.

As he became more debilitated, he also became more vulnerable. Always in the past he could easily stick up for himself, but now he needed help. I was just a lot faster to his defense than he was. Was this because he was slow on the draw or that he didn't expect to be in that position? Or was there some other reason I'd yet to fathom?

My doctor brain was thinking, *Come on, you know this always happens.*

My wife brain said, "You have to support and protect your husband. He is counting on you."

The mother reprimanded, "You cannot be mean to the child whose father has cancer. You have to be a better mother."

The Blessing Known as "Bob"

"Never miss a chance to say yes!" – Lisa McClure

It was November when Bob called. "I'm coming down next Saturday to help you," he told me.

"Bob, I really don't know that I need any help." I answered, slightly surprised.

"Have you closed up the motor home for the winter yet?"

"No, not yet." I hadn't even remembered we owned a motor home. Thom had always done all the mechanical things related to it.

"I'll be down after lunch. We'll work all afternoon, you'll feed me dinner, and then I'll head home."

"Bob, that is so nice, but I don't know what else to have you do besides the motor home."

"Make a list."

"Make a list?" I asked, slightly confused.

"Yeah, by the time I get there you'll have a list," like he knew I had a big secret list.

"Ok, Bob," I acquiesced, "if you say so."

"Yep. Make a list." Then he hung up.

By the time Bob arrived, I had an eight-hour list. People were always asking me if they could do anything for me, but I could never come up with anything. Somehow knowing he was coming and having a few days to plan for it allowed me to see how many things I really could use help with. The truth is that I was challenged just getting a meal together. There were things that ordinarily I could do, but now I had no energy to do. Everything seemed so insignificant in the face of Thom's cancer.

Bob arrived with more energy than three ordinary people. Thom wasn't real bad yet so he and Bob started on the motor home together.

After about an hour, Thom was exhausted and frozen. He came in and asked me to help. I put him under the electric blanket and finished up the motor home with Bob. Basically, I just followed his instructions.

After knocking off a few more things on the list, Bob looked at a slight sag in our gutters. "Did you clean those out yet? If they freeze with the leaves and water in there, the weight could pull the gutters right off the house."

Why didn't I know that? Not only that, I couldn't remember the last time I had cleaned them out. I had forgotten I even had gutters.

It was getting dark as Bob and I cleaned out the gutters. I steadied the ladder and he pulled out all the leaves and black slimy debris. He was scooping it out with his bare hands and throwing it down on the ground. However, I was down there holding the ladder and half of it kept landing on my head. I kept asking him to be more careful.

Finally I yelled up to him. "Jesus Christ, Bob! I'm so glad you came down here to help me and decided to start shitting on my head. Are you trying to work out some pent up childhood resentment with me or what? I remember you throwing rocks up at me in that tree in your yard when I was five or six and me pitching them right back down at you."

We laughed ourselves silly talking about our childhood memories as we worked in the cold. Funny how you never realize how important those childhood bonding experiences really are.

I told him how I used to go over to our Nana's each week to do her hair before she went to play Bingo at church on Friday night. I was at Nana's. He was in Vietnam.

Nana loved Bob. He was easily her favorite grandchild. She always talked about him while I curled her short white hair. She taught me her Dippity-do routine. Slather the shellac gel on each set of hair, then wind it over the 5-cent diameter roller as tight as possible and hold it in place with a long pink plastic pick.

Usually she would read *LIFE* magazine while I was rolling her hair. There were these incredible pictures from Vietnam week after week. They scared the heck out of me, and they always made her cry and carry on about Bob. She was worried sick about him being over there.

After putting her hair up, I'd put on the portable hair dryer and play a few rounds of canasta with her to take her mind off Bob. I was telling him all this while we worked. He loved hearing Nana stories. She sure said a lot of prayers for Bob, and a lot of rosaries and novenas too.

We never underestimated the power of prayer. We both thought she probably saved his life with those prayers.

In a way, Bob saved my life with all the help and the energy infusion. He definitely saved my gutters. We reverently called these lists, "A Bob's List." So thoughtful and helpful.

As more and more things fell off Thom's plate, I picked them up. I did all the shopping, meal planning, cooking, driving the kids to and from appointments, and general organizing. Thom withdrew more and more from the routine of everyday life.

He didn't become depressed, but he became more thoughtful, or I should say full of thoughts—incredible thoughts. As my day became filled with mundane necessities, Thom's was overflowing with spiritual essentials.

In the shifts we were making to move our lives forward, the significant ones that he was making almost went unnoticed. The change was only evident when I looked back over several weeks or months, but when I did, it was astounding.

Of course, the intangible is so difficult to see but here is how it happened.

Most days, I came home from work earlier than I had when Thom was well. He would be stretched out on the green velvet couch, his head resting comfortably on the wide low arm facing the fireplace, his eyes closed.

Quietly, I would creep down the two steps from the kitchen into the great room. Despite my stealth, as I neared his head he would always open his eyes to greet me. After repeating this scenario several times, I realized that he had not been napping at all, but meditating. Since we both believed in the power of guided imagery, I assumed he was focusing on strengthening his immune system or something else related to his cancer.

Boy, was I wrong. (As often as I was wrong in this process, you'd think I would have gotten used to it!) One afternoon, he watched silently as I kissed him on the forehead and sat down next to him on the rocker.

"What were you thinking about today, honey?"

It wasn't cancer. It wasn't chemo. He turned and looked straight at me and said, "I think that most of my life I took things too personally."

Where did that come from? Apparently, he didn't notice my surprise because he kept right on talking.

"Life is just about the lessons, you know? Just learning the lessons."

Where is this coming from? And where is this going?

"You know?" He asked as if we have had this conversation before and he is just refreshing my memory. "Just learning the lessons, not getting wrapped up in the pain that might come as you go through the learning process."

It was a good thing I was sitting down because I could have been knocked over with a few more heavy insights like those. Looking back, I am not sure why I was so surprised that these thoughts were on his mind. There is no telling what a person facing his own death would think about. I mean, you and I can spend a few minutes of deep thought about it, but then we can get up and walk away back into the kitchen, back into our healthy reality.

This switch can't happen to a person for whom health is a distant memory, not to a person with cancer, not to a person contemplating the end of his life. Surely if anyone would think about looking back on life and its meaning, it would be Thom. He was the death and dying expert. He took all the courses. He studied it. He wrote papers on it. He had gone through it with patients, family and friends. Now he was looking into the face of death again, only this time it was looking back at him.

Once I tuned into Thom's new perspective, I sought him out with questions each afternoon. I looked forward to coming home each day, making a pot of tea, and talking to my husband about his daily musings.

One afternoon, while sipping our tea, he was reclining on the green velvet couch and I was sitting in the rocker, and there was a lull in the conversation. As I gazed over at Thom, he was staring intently at the stones of the chimney above the fireplace lost in thought.

What did he see in there? Was there something magical about the pattern of the dry-laid granite stones? Did it reveal some previously unforeseen mysteries?

I too started staring at the fireplace. Somehow I had never really appreciated the beauty in each individual stone and its relationship to all the others.

Funny how you can look at something for years and then one day it suddenly looks completely different. You could start out at the bottom layers with one thing on your mind and, as your eyes moved up each row of irregular granite brick-size stones, the idea changed and then changed again. Some connected or corresponding idea crept in and altered the whole focus of your thoughts.

Or maybe it was the other way around. As you looked up, more and more thoughts evaporated to reveal a more essential truth. After a few trips up that thirty-foot chimney, you could be on another planet.

I was studying Thom's face for a clue to understanding the secrets of the fireplace stones when he turned and looked at me as if he heard my nonverbal questions.

"Today I've been thinking about reflection and introspection."

Okay get ready.

"I think people should actually take some time every year or so to look at themselves. I mean *really* look at themselves, in a way that redefines them. You know, upgrade their definition of themselves."

"I am not sure exactly what you mean."

"Well, when you are young, your parents or grandparents define you by telling you that you are a good boy because you did this or that. Or they tell you that you're lazy or stupid or you are a bad boy or any of a thousand other painful things parents can say. If you're not careful, you could take that to heart and incorporate that into your idea of who you are, even if it doesn't fit you. Pretty soon you could lose sight of who or what you really are now. As adults, we should be defining our own selves and then updating that definition regularly."

"You mean, like, what has life taught me about myself and my beliefs? Have I changed? Should I change? What do I want to become? What do I want to let go of and what do I want to hold onto? This is me now. This is what is important now? How will I accomplish these new goals?"

"Exactly. Maybe that is why so many people get to the end of their lives and ask, 'Is this all there is?'"

"You heard that from patients?"

He nodded, looking sad for the first time in this conversation. "Too many times to count."

One of the examples Thom shared was how his paternal grandmother always had an intense dislike for him. Charming as a child can be, she never warmed up to him. He was confused and hurt by this as a child, but let it go. Years after her death and with an adult and psychoanalytic perspective he understood it. It wasn't Thom, the cute little black curly-haired child she didn't like, but what he symbolized.

Thom's father, who was 100% German, married a woman who had some Jewish heritage. Thom's grandparents had the marriage annulled because Thom's mother was too young, but when his parents were of age they went out and got married again. The grandmother never got over the idea that she had a somewhat Jewish grandson and held it against Thom.

When you think of it, there are so many ideas in or about people that have nothing to with who they really are. I guess that is why it is so important to get that definition clear in your own mind.

My friend, Bonnie, used to say that Thom was one of the smartest people she had ever met. *Why didn't I know that?* It took me to this point in our marriage to really appreciate my husband's fine mind. I was so grateful for those afternoon discussions. They gave me such insight into Thom. Of course, it would often take me several mental trips up the fireplace to really wrap my mind all the way around those thoughts.

The Drumming Begins

"Ease on into it." – Marilyn Marianni,
her advice on what to say to a dying person

Sometime in the fall, my second cousin, Ric, re-entered Thom's life. He was our landscape architect when we built our house.

Near the beginning of that project, Thom and Ric realized they shared a love of Native American religion. Come to find out, Ric, who is part Native American, is a shaman. For years he had been studying with well-known shamans to learn the healing arts of American Indians.

He and Thom started talking about the healing powers of drumming and how it is an integral part of Native American ceremonies. When Ric asked Thom where *his* drum was, Thom told him it was in California. He had lent his drum to his best friend and told the friend to "send it back when he was finished with it."

Thom was now on his second round of chemo. The first chemo treatment we'd pursued had done nothing to halt the cancer. In fact, things were worse than ever before. The cancer had spread to his whole body by this time.

That's where things stood with Thom when Ric started coming by. He gave Thom one of his handmade drums and told Thom to "give it back when he was done with it." The drum was about 12" around with dried deer hide stretched tight over a 3" wide maple circle held down by rawhide laces strung on the back into a rawhide handle. The front was a light blond color.

Thom drew Native American symbols on it: an eagle feather and his chosen animal spirit, a snake.

It was that drum that started everything.

For the first few months, it sat quietly on a chair next to the bookcase in the great room and got little use. Then I guess I told Ric things were not going well for Thom or maybe he just heard it through the small town grapevine. About then, Ric started showing up on Tuesday afternoons, regularly.

At first, it seemed novel and thoughtful, but as Ric continued to show up on Tuesday afternoons, it was evident that something more than visiting was going on.

At that time, Tuesday was the one day I worked an eight-hour day, so I wasn't at home when they were together. (It was the only time when I was at work that I didn't feel guilty leaving Thom because when I would get home, he was always in a great mood.)

Thom and Ric had some Indian connectedness that was very beneficial to Thom. It was something so intimately spiritual that I never really asked about it. But later, I became curious. I wanted to know. What did they do in there? How did it help Thom? How did it happen?

I asked Ric for help understanding. He subsequently tried to explain to me what he and Thom did in those afternoons. Now I will try to explain it to you, but honestly it's not going to be easy. What went on between them is like trying to explain another culture. Furthermore, there are no words in the English language that relate to the ceremonies of Native Americans. So it's like speaking another language as well.

This is how I understood what Ric told me. For years Thom and I had spent time in linear thinking (you know, A + B = C), and in running our business and our family, making dinner and taking care of the children. Now there was a large paradigm shift. Ric said they were pursuing non-linear, non-definitive thought processes.

Thom was moving toward some point, some place deep yet away from the usual awareness. His process peeled away layers to reveal the core of "it all." There are no words to describe the meaning, nor the process. I can only call it a transformation.

In American culture, we see life as being linear. The longer the line, the more we lived. American Indians see life as circular. The circle is complete at puberty. After that, the circle just expands and grows in all directions to incorporate all of life's experiences. Life's last experience is death. When you die, your circle is already complete. You die in a state of wholeness. The fuller you experience each moment of your life the greater the circle. The wisdom here is that you are then prepared for death.

Crazy Horse, that great American Indian sage, is famous for saying, "Today is a good day to die, for all things in my life are present."

This type of thinking is why my discussion with Ric was so difficult to understand, but here is what went on.

Each afternoon, they started by burning sage to clear the spiritual air. This is called "smudging."

Then, they would drum together. They each had one of Ric's handmade, deer hide drums in one hand and a "beater" (a stick with a deer hide ball stuffed with horse hair attached to one end) in the other. The drum beating accompanied a variety of songs and chants that they would do together. This somehow brought them in harmony with each other and with the spiritual world.

Initially, Ric worked with Thom's energy fields to balance them out. He would concentrate on his legs so Thom would continue to be able to walk despite the cancer that was then in his spine. It also helped Thom get to a more comfortable place with his pain. Ric explained that it's like yoga, enabling a person to get to a transcendental state.

Thom was a willing and capable student for Ric. Thanks to his years as a therapist, and because he was Thom, he had strong desire and insight. Therefore, he was able to move right along with Ric "between worlds." He would travel out of his body and this concrete reality of everyday life to move right into the spiritual reality.

Ric said there are many ways to do this, but mostly they "journeyed" together through Ric's guided meditation. This is where one person takes another on an imaginary journey to another place where something healing happens that can be discussed on their return. The experience can then be a way to gain insight and understanding into where the person is in their life.

They also performed a pipe ceremony, which I never did understand, but it worked for them.

The greatest benefit for Thom was to be able to reach a place of deep peace—a place outside of pain and away from thoughts of everyday life and any superficiality. Sometimes they worked together to tie up loose ends of his past that he was working on. Sometimes they would stay in "the beauty of now."

There are many names for this mindset or mindfulness, but here is how I understand it. This state is an intense sensing of all that is presently occurring at one moment in time, in one thing. For example, take a tree. They would try to feel everything that the tree is feeling, including the sunlight and the wind on its leaves, the chlorophyll being formed there, the water as it moves from the roots to the leaves, the wind swaying in the branches, the feeling of a bird alighting on its branches, the relationship of that tree to all the other trees, even the sounds of the forest and the river as the tree would detect them.

It is awareness on many different levels. It is a state of knowing that everything that was present in that moment was connected to everything else, even themselves. These experiences made Thom very content on every level.

Fuck Cancer

"There is a lot to learn in life." – Roberta Moran,
when talking about death and dying

So many different realities were buzzing in the same house. If it were possible to hear an energy field around our house, it would have been crackling.

Thom was on his spiritual quest. Caitlin launched into her high school and friends. I was struggling with the balance of the wife, mother and doctor roles, and Justine was just plain old pissed off on a daily basis. Her life now sucked.

One afternoon when she and I were alone at home, we stepped out of her room down a couple steps onto the bridge when in the middle of it Justine stopped.

"Mom?"

"Yeah, honey?"

"I am really mad and want to use the F-word."

"You do?" Where was this coming from and where was it going? "Who do you want to use the F-word on?"

"Cancer," she squints her deep brown eyes at me to accentuate her resolve, "I want to use the F-word on cancer."

In a flash, I weighed the power of the F-word and the power of cancer, the importance of those two words together, as well as the power of releasing anger in a child who had kept it bottled up for far too long. I took a deep breath.

"I think in this case we should make an exception to our no-swearing policy."

Her eyebrows flew up unexpectedly. What should she do next? We looked at each other while that idea sunk in.

"Fuck" she said rather flatly. I waited patiently, surely there had to be more than that.

"Fuck cancer." She said with gusto. She stopped and looked at me expectantly.

"Say it again, Justine. Say it louder."

She went to the middle of the bridge, grabbed the handrail, stood with her feet apart, threw her head back and screamed, "Fuck cancer. Fuck cancer! *Fuck cancer!*"

She paused and looked at me. *Was this an invitation?* Without hesitation, I joined in.

"Fuck cancer."

"FUCK DAD'S CANCER," she shot off like fireworks into the air.

"FUCK THOM'S CANCER."

"FUCK EVERYONE'S CANCER," I added to the fireworks.

Then we were on a roll chanting in unison at the top of our lungs, "FUCK CANCER, FUCK CANCER, FUCK CANCER, FUCK CANCER, FUCK CANCER, FUCK CANCER," over and over until our anger was spent.

Exhilarated, we stood looking at each other with a "what's next?" look on our faces. I mean, really. What do you do after you have fucked cancer?

Next, I flipped up my right middle finger and Justine looked at me surprised as I flipped up my left middle finger and held them above my head in my best *en garde* stance. She immediately realized she was being challenged to a "swear finger duel." Ah, yes! One more way to fuck cancer before we were through.

She quickly flipped up her little middle fingers and accepted the challenge. The swear finger sword fight was engaged. Back and forth we went on the bridge arms and fingers extended in grand Peter-Pan style.

There were several stabs of tickling among all the giggling as we flew around. For those minutes, no words were spoken, but much was communicated. When all the anger was spent, we collapsed on the floor and hugged with all our might.

As we walked down the stairs arm-in-arm, our bodies relaxed and flexible for the first time in a long time, a thought occurred to me.

What if Justine goes to school tomorrow and tells someone there, like in show-and-tell, about what just went on here? How would it sound to someone that she and I were swearing, the worst swearing, about cancer? Would they understand? Could they understand why this was so important for me to do with my daughter?

"You know, Justine, I am really glad we had a chance to do this."

"Yeah, me too," she agreed.

"But I don't think we should tell anyone else about this, okay? I mean, no one could possibly understand what this is all about unless they had been here with us. You know? They might get the wrong idea."

"Mom! Duh!" she answered. Her tone of voice told me what she really wanted to say was "No shit, Mom!" But after all, we had a strict no-swearing policy.

The Truth

"The goal is to live in such a way that our lives
will prove worth dying for." – *Forrest Church*

It seems almost sacrilegious to mention the negative aspects of a person who has cancer or is dead, but the truth is, we all have weaknesses and flaws. We keep them well hidden and for darn sure we don't advertise them, but as long as we are human beings, we are going to make mistakes. For most of us, not only is it the best way to learn, it's the *only* way we learn—the only way we incorporate life's lessons into understanding ourselves.

Over the years, many patients have confided in me truths about their lives and feelings that they have never shared with anyone else. Confessing these painful personal histories allows us to work together to gain insight and understanding into our deepest self. Through this process of self-revelation and self-discovery, we can become significantly better people.

Not surprisingly, this process is most often initiated by a crisis. Suddenly, everything in our life goes to hell in a handbasket—everything as we knew it is in pieces and, like Humpty Dumpty, it can't be put back together in the same way again. Few people really change the way they think or the way they do things without real pain motivating them. So it was with Thom.

Most importantly, the changes he made gave us the three best years of our lives together. This is why I can share with you a painful part of his story.

Moving from California in 1998 was a major change in Thom's life. He left his psychotherapy practice of 28 years. He left his friends. He left his family. He left all his favorite restaurants, gourmet food shops and boutique clothing shops on Melrose, and the beautiful California beaches where he loved to surf.

In short, he left his physical, financial and emotional comfort zone—all to move back to Connecticut to be with my entire (dysfunctional) family.

We should have known better than to have a family member build our house. It was only later that we learned of the tremendous financial and emotional stresses my brother was under. Our house was literally the last house he built before his business went under, and it ran many months behind schedule and way over budget.

Meanwhile, the four of us (me, Thom and the two girls), two lab puppies and a very unhappy cat were living in our 28-foot motor home. We were parked and plugged in at my parents' pool. All of our belongings and clothes were in storage in California, but we were promised to be in our house by September.

August rolled around and the house was barely half-way finished. It was clear how impossible it would be to continue to live at my parents' pool and send the kids to school from our motor home, so we rented a house, bought new beds, winter coats and whatever clothes I could find from the local consignment shops.

It felt luxurious to go to our own room and sleep in a real bed. That happiness was short-lived however. Our house in California didn't sell. The house we were building wasn't finished when our building loan came due and our savings alone were not enough to complete our new home. Suddenly, we had the equivalent of three mortgages running consecutively (not to mention the motor home payments), and only one income coming in. After nine months of that, we had no savings left and no available cash.

Thom became more and more agitated as the weeks went by.

"You focus on making the new medical practice profitable and I'll take over managing the house."

In theory, it was a good idea because if I had grasped how financially strapped we had become I would have been crippled at work, but the day he told me we had to sit down and have a serious financial discussion, I knew we were in deep trouble.

One look at his grim face drained of all color said it was bad. He kept opening and clenching his fists as he laid out how dismal our money problems were. I was trying to take it in, but honestly it did not register. Never in my life had I been on the financial bottom.

"What are we going to do?"

"We can borrow ourselves into even more significant debt, although I don't know who would even lend us any money at this point. We are new here and have a new business, an unfinished house and a shit-load of debt."

Okay, I was getting the bleak picture, but I wasn't ready for his next statement. "I think we should consider bankruptcy."

"What?" I croaked.

Seriously talking about bankruptcy was one of those conversations I wish I could forget, but there were so few options left. Eventually we borrowed a small amount of money from our parents. We moved into an unfinished house in the spring of 1999, but had walls, a roof, running water and electricity and were grateful at that.

Shortly after that, the California house sold and the tide had turned. However, Thom's spirits were not bouncing back the way that mine did. Somehow I totally discounted some crucial aspects of the male ego. Money is important in ways that I had not considered. The "provider of the family" and all that mentality is still deeply ingrained.

It was one of the few things that we looked at very differently. Thom felt tremendously more demoralized by the whole process than I did. Honestly, I didn't even notice.

Sometime during the fall, I began noticing strange things about Thom's behavior. Several times he got irate and fell into fits of temper with me or the girls over stupid little stuff. The girls had each gotten a few doses of "the Dad in a rotten mood." There were a couple of dinner parties we went to where he made some very inappropriate comments (the kind where I wanted to kick him under the table to get him to stop talking). Several of our new friends stopped talking to us. A few times he missed appointments with patients, which was totally unlike him. He was usually extremely compulsive about being on time.

Then I started finding empty highball glasses on the floor under the chair where he had been watching TV the night before. Prior to this he was pretty much only a California wine drinker.

I asked him if he was drinking every day, which he denied. It never even crossed my mind that he would lie to me. I wrote a lot of this behavior off as him being stressed and not sleeping well. I gave him the benefit of the doubt until the day I came home unexpectedly early.

He didn't hear me come home because he was in the office over the garage with the TV blaring. When I walked in on him, he tried to hide the glass, like a kid with his hand in the cookie jar. I grabbed the glass and took a whiff—gin. This was 2:00 in the afternoon, and I knew he had a counseling appointment later that same afternoon.

"That does it," I said between clenched teeth. Storming downstairs and into the kitchen, I threw the glass into the sink. With both hands holding on to the small counter in front of the sink I stared out the kitchen window. The peaceful setting out there was not what I was seeing at that moment. What was streaming across my consciousness was all the odd incidents of the last few months, and worst of all now they all made sense.

Each incident by itself was not that significant, but now that I was tapped into them, I saw them for what they truly were: excuses to drink. All the frustrations, disappointments, financial challenges—anything at all, really—were an excuse to get toasted.

Shuffling into the atrium in a daze, I did not even see where I was going because all I saw was Thom's inappropriate behaviors playing like a video camera before my eyes. My heart was racing up in my throat, and my mouth was dry. I was in full battle mode, adrenalized, ready to fight the tiger in the room.

Thom crept silently into the atrium after me. Too furious to speak, I looked at him with dagger eyes pinning him to that spot and daring him to speak. He stood silently, arms hanging at his side, looking down at the rug as I paced back and forth, as if I had lost my way in my own house.

"You disgust me," I began. "I am ashamed of your behavior, and I'm ashamed of *you*."

He said nothing. "You know what? I don't even want to be anywhere near you. You can cry and whine about 'poor you' and all that's happened to you financially and otherwise, but you know what? I don't give a damn any more. What makes your life so darn miserable? Is this all about money? Or the house? If it is, I don't have to live here. I can live in a goddamn tent."

Somewhere in my mind it registered that he was miserable, but I didn't care. "If this house is stressing you out to the point of making you a drunk, let's sell it. Let's sell it today."

Never in our married life had he seen me this side of me. In a time warp, my mind raced like a freight train at 100 miles an hour.

"I don't like the choices you have been making. I have interceded with the children, but I am embarrassed by the way you have come down on Justine lately. It's just not right. Now you are going to see a patient shortly, and although you are not drunk—well what do I know, you may very well *be* drunk! But the fact that you would even *consider* drinking before counseling a patient means that you have sunk to some new low in your life. You are out of control. But you know what? I AM NOT. I will not put up with your pathetic bullshit any longer."

He was frozen in that one spot by my anger and his guilt. I was on a roll. I saw each inappropriate behavior of his for what it really was: an act of self-indulgence. Each one was a retreat from me, a retreat from our life together. Withdrawal from our time for each other and from the girls. With each and every drink, he chose to withdraw. It fueled my ire.

Up until now I had put up with it all because somehow I had convinced myself it was a phase he was going through. I told myself it was a coping technique for rough times that in some way I was responsible for, at least to some degree. As the "good wife," I put up with it and looked the other way.

Things would get better and then he (and we) would be better also. I would just have to ride it out. Maybe we would be better for having gone through such a difficult time. But, no.

This was an all-too-thin veil for the bold truth of alcoholism: Addiction first. Everything and everyone else, second.

Somehow the realization that I would be second-best to a drink made me want to puke. Never, never, *never* would I live my life as second-best to alcohol.

Way too many lines had been crossed, for far too long. My empathy, understanding and forgiveness were gone. Period. Something had to give and it wasn't going to be me. There must have been some dammed-up place somewhere deep inside my psyche that broke loose at that moment, because things came gushing out of my mouth that I didn't know were in there.

"You know what? I deserve better. You owe me better than this. If you can't do it, then I want you out of my life. All those times that you told me you weren't drinking or drunk when I thought you were—I believed you. I believed you over my own self! What a fool I was. I was pretty sure you were drunk, but somehow you convinced me you weren't. I doubted myself. I loved you and I let you make me doubt my own self! How sick is that?"

I was pacing again, thinking *How the heck did I let this get to this point?*

Then it hit me. Pointing my index finger like a gun, I fired, "You knew I would, didn't you? You knew you could get away with it. Deep down inside, you had me sized up perfectly. You knew I would let you talk me out of believing reality. You *counted* on taking advantage of me. Didn't you? You knew my weakness was loving you and you took advantage of that love."

His silence let me know I had hit the bull's eye. I stopped pacing.

"Well that's over now. It's on my terms now or you are out." I jerked my thumb over my shoulder at the front door as I looked at him with more daggers. He felt the stabbing.

I wanted to call him that name, the name he knew he deserved. I wanted to hurt him with the truth, and so I said it. "I should have known better than to trust a drunk!"

Suddenly, I began to think about other times and situations when he might have been drunk and I didn't suspect a thing—times perhaps when he was alone or with my family or with the girls. Oh my God, the girls.

"I trusted you with the lives of our children. You were probably drunk when you were driving them around town too, weren't you?"

He shrunk down as if he would like to climb under the rug. I had just discovered the dirtiest truth about him.

"You bastard! How could you? You drove our children around when you were drunk? You endangered the lives of our children? And for what reason would that be? Because you had to have a drink? Because you had to escape your oh-so-pitiful life?"

I wanted to hit him. I wanted to lash out. I wanted to make some sense out of this insanity. There could be none, I realized. There was no way out. There were no words that he could say, no possible excuses nor explanations.

"Get out of my face. Get out of my bedroom. Get out of my life. You can live in the motor home. You can go back to California if you want. For all I care, you can go to hell."

Dead silence.

There we were, two adults who had loved and supported each other all those years, now squared off as if in a boxing ring. He was down for the count, and I didn't care. I turned my back on him and looked out the window. I could hear the referee counting down as if he was a loud drum beating. Or maybe there was a jackhammer attacking concrete outside my front door. Bizarre. I then realized that the beating was coming from inside my own head. My heart was attacking my head.

I took slow deep breaths so I could try to think. My mind was racing in a conversation with my heart.

Marianne, if you kick him out, he has nowhere to go and no one to go to. The nice Marianne.

So what? It was his choice. He chose his addiction over me and our family, time after time. Screw him! The not-nice Marianne.

Do you really want this to be the end?

If he drinks, yes!

And if he stops? What if he actually turns around and chooses you and the girls over his drinking? What if he is successful?

Fat chance. I'll believe that when I see it.

I was imagining what telling the girls would be like and what it would do to them. I was so engrossed in my internal struggle that I had forgotten Thom was there.

"You're right, Marianne," he said slowly, softly, his voice flat. "I am ashamed of myself."

He had never said so little, but he didn't need to say anything more. We both knew what would be next. We both had counseled enough drunks to know what had to be done.

"Alright," I said. "You know the deal. Thirty meetings in thirty days. Any drinking and you are out for good. I mean it. No leniency. No second chances. Period."

He nodded.

"Since we don't have enough money for me to really kick you out of the house, you can live in the office over the garage." I went to the closet, grabbed a pillow and blanket, and threw them at him.

"That's what you get."

"Can I still cook and take care of the girls?"

"Yes. And I will be civil to you in front of the girls, but you are to have no other communication with me."

He shook his head. He understood.

"Oh, and don't come into my bedroom or my bathroom while I'm in there either. You work around my schedule." I said it like a dare. He got the point.

Work was my escape and my nourishment. Home was a frosty trip to the North Pole. Thom would cook dinner and I left him to clean up. Afterward, I would retreat to the living room and he would go back up to the office. No communication. I put the girls to bed at night. He sent them to school in the morning.

Like many alcoholics, Thom started out by going to AA meetings in towns other than our own. Morning, lunch and evening, he tried them all. Some days he went to two meetings. Each day he would tell me where he went. I would listen, just listen, and look at him. No words of encouragement, no condemnations. Just a look.

Thirty days is a long time to live with someone and not really communicate. I wasn't sure he could pull himself together and remain sober. I was pretty angry those first few weeks, so I didn't really care to be on his team.

After the thirty days, I was significantly calmer and in a more receptive mood. He came to me and apologized. He promised his drinking days were over. He solemnly swore to strive each day to be a better husband and better father. This he promised to accomplish with every effort he could possibly muster. If at any time he slipped, he would expect to pack his bags for good. In the meantime, he wanted to continue going to meetings. He felt they really helped him. (Funny how he found some of the best meetings right here in our own town.)

He seemed different in small, but significant, ways. He was enjoying cooking again. He looked forward to his time with the girls. He was more engaged in what they were doing. He joked and teased them like he used to do. They loved it. Hearing them all laugh together warmed my heart. He looked and acted happy. Life seemed to have purpose again. He was focused. His old confident self returned, just more worn around the edges.

After the thirty days, he asked if he could move back into the bedroom. I wanted to say no, but how could I when he had clearly kept his end of the agreement?

I didn't know if we could put our relationship together again. It could never be what it was before, that much I knew. Maybe it could come together in some other way that would be as good. Was that possible?

I was unsure of where we were headed, but he clearly had been sober for thirty days, and there was the promise of a sober life ahead. I was willing to see where this would take us.

He put the old pillow and blanket back in the hall closet as I held the door open.

Thom really enjoyed going to the meetings. He said that everyone there was like him. They each struggled to deal with their addictions and regain control of their lives.

He became the model AA person. Actually, he continued going to three or four meetings each week, to the point that it was getting annoying! Every time I wanted to schedule something as a family, he was at a meeting.

His favorite was the Friday night meeting at the Congregational Church right down the road. He was assigned the job of setting up. This included buying coffee and cookies, and then setting up the chairs in the church hall before the meeting.

He would always buy fancy coffee and cookies from the bakery next to our office. It tickled me to see him giggling in anticipation of treating the other alcoholics to something special at the meeting.

Since he went to set up before I got home from work and Caitlin got home from high school late on Fridays, he usually took Justine with him. She liked the routine too.

Together they would line up all the chairs and then go next door to Tony's, the country market next to the church. Thom always bought her some chocolates.

Tony's was where I would meet them on my way home from work. Thom told Justine that the meetings were a self-help group where people came together to work on their problems and better themselves. I loved that definition, so true to the point. It wasn't until years after he died that she learned that the group was for recovering alcoholics.

Thom never "slipped," not even when he had his cancer. He remained true to his word. He literally tried every day to be a better person, a better husband, and a better father. He was always saying, "it's never too late to be the best you can possibly be."

It was a miraculous experience to witness him becoming his best self like he had promised. He certainly won a newfound respect from his wife.

I was also proud of myself for waiting to see what would happen between us. Initially, I didn't think he could do it. Maybe I wasn't even sure that I wanted him to, but as I slowly let go of my anger I was able to see a sincerity, desire and drive that made me proud of Thom. Sort of proving that he was made of "the right stuff."

In some ways, what I learned was equally important. Up until that time in my life, I had thought that love was the most powerful emotion.

Love could cure all, heal all, supply the energy to surmount any obstacle, and was the single most powerful force in the universe.

But after going through all this with Thom, I started to think that forgiveness was equally as powerful. It was much more challenging for me to forgive.

Movies are full of righteous indignation and retaliation. Someone, usually an unsuspecting and undeserving person, is done a grievous wrong. The rest of the movie is how the bad guys get their well-deserved payback. They sure are fun to watch, but living with that righteous indignation is an insidious experience. It eats away at you. You become less than you were to begin with. It can corrupt your own moral fiber.

So, to me, forgiveness is more challenging and therefore maybe even more powerful. You have to get to a place of making room for forgiveness first. Maybe that's when love can come back in.

The Realization

"You can't beat death. I know I tried." – Sandra Horan

I wrote earlier about our magnificent grand piano, but I didn't tell you how we got it.

It was some time in the fall of 2002, a few months after Thom was diagnosed, that Caitlin's piano teacher, Mrs. Havery, sent a note home to us. I read it out loud to Thom.

> Caitlin shows real promise on the piano. Unfortunately, her ability to practice at home on only a keyboard is holding her back. Would it be possible to rent or even buy a piano?

"Oh my God," I said to Thom, holding the note limply in my hand. "We have to buy a piano," we said in unison.

We looked in the newspaper and we spoke to friends. Finally, we took the advice of our local piano tuner. He recommended a man in West Hartford who re-built Steinways.

Yes, he knew we were not going to buy a Steinway, new or re-built, but this man, Dave, had a showroom next to his shop where he sold only one other new piano: a Ritmüller.

The piano was made in Germany and the soundboard came from Korea and, in our piano tuner's opinion, the quality of the sound it produced was second only to a Steinway.

We met Dave in his workshop on a Saturday afternoon. The Steinways were magnificent. He showed them off by playing "Tea for Two," a favorite of mine, which I still remember as sounding the best I have ever heard it.

He let Caitlin play any piano she wanted and of course she went for the Steinways. She played on a seven-foot grand and a ten-foot concert grand. What a delight to hear your child play an instrument like that.

Finally, she came around to playing the Ritmüller. We all liked the sound exceedingly well. We were talking about the colors they came in and the size we would like.

The next thing I knew Thom said, "We'll take the mahogany seven-footer."

Just like that! Even though he had made similar quick decisions many times before, it never ceased to amaze me how quickly he could come to a decision. Personally I like to sleep on any big decisions, but not Thom. He weighed the options and made his decision. Period. Done.

As we went back to Dave's office to write up the bill of sale, we walked past a large Steinway that he had taken apart and he showed Caitlin and Justine exactly what he was doing. It was tedious work, an obvious labor of love.

As the girls continued to watch Dave, I spied a balcony upstairs and asked him if I could go up there. Up in the loft, there were hand-turned wooden bowls, oil paintings and watercolors hung on the walls as if there had been an art show there recently.

"Hey, Dave," I called down to him. "Whose gallery is this up here? This artwork is outrageous."

"Oh, that's mine," he said, peeking out from under the Steinway lid. He came upstairs and told me about his art work as I held each piece up for Thom to admire. He was on a piano stool downstairs leaning back against the wall obviously too tired to climb up the stairs, but he enjoyed the artwork nonetheless.

Then Dave leaned over to me and in a conspiratorial tone asked, "What's wrong with him? He doesn't look well."

I looked down from our balcony vantage point to see my bald, pale husband sitting on a piano stool, propped up against the wall. I turned and looked at Dave. "He's got cancer," I said flatly.

"Is he going to make it?" he asked.

"No, Dave." I said slowly, my doctor brain responding truthfully. "He's not." We both looked down on Thom as if we knew—like gods looking down from heaven—we knew Thom's outcome, but were powerless to change it.

"You know the really hard part?" I asked Dave.

He looked at me as if he wasn't really sure he wanted to know, but he nodded.

"I'm the only one who knows it at this point. I know he's not going to make it. And nobody else knows."

I don't remember what he said or if he said anything at all, but the look on his face told me that he too wanted *not* to know.

I guess it's just too much for most people to deal with. *Oh here is so-and-so and they are dying. They will soon cease to exist.*

We live in a society that is so focused on the future. It's uncomfortable when you know that this person you are talking to is *not* going to be in the future. What do you say? Do you start talking about their death or what? People really freak out in that situation.

Here I was, telling a basic stranger that my husband is going to die in the near future. I wanted to tell someone, but poor Dave looked like a dump truck just backed up and unloaded a ton of bricks on him.

Still, it took time for all of me to accept my own words—that Thom was not going to beat the cancer. Maybe it was that wife-doctor thing going on again. Sometimes, in the day-to-day care, I could put aside the doctor knowledge. But then it would come back and slap me full-force in the face.

It happened again when I was shopping for Christmas. Quietly passing through the aisles, I was unconsciously scratching things off my list of potential gifts for Thom. Nothing from the cooking aisles, my staple gift area for the last 16 years. He was barely eating. No swimwear for our annual trip to Puerto Rico. He wasn't going to Puerto Rico anymore. No sports equipment or new racquetball sneakers. There was no working out or thinking of how to be fit.

There wasn't anything he needed and there wasn't anything I could think of that he might need or want for the foreseeable future, because the future just wasn't going to be that long.

No sense in wasting any money, my subconscious was saying. *He's not going to make it.* Waiting in line at the checkout stand, I started to sweat as if someone had turn the heat up really high. Unzipping my down coat, I peered through a narrow tunnel at the checkout lady as she took my credit card. She seemed to be talking to me from another room or maybe she was speaking a foreign language, because she didn't make any sense to me as I watched her mouth move. I grabbed my bags and focused on the exit door. My legs were melting, yet I was moving in the right direction. My feet felt like I had moon boots on or maybe the exit floor was made of marshmallows.

This must be what a diabetic feels during an insulin reaction, my doctor mind observed.

Keep calm. Carry on. Get outside. Get to the cold air before you faint or puke.

My packages were strewn on the sidewalk as I propped myself up with one arm on the cinder block wall, the other pulling my coat off. Slow deep breaths, in through the nose out the mouth—just like in yoga class. *Slow down, heart. Slow down, guts. You can do it.*

The freezing air cooled my fevered body and mind. But what would soothe my soul?

I was caught in an avalanche of emotions and physical reactions to the awareness I could no longer keep contained. It was as if a huge trapdoor had been opened and I was being swept down into a dark place that I always knew was there, but now was helpless to avoid.

Some place, some deep-down place, maybe in the DNA of my every cell, I felt the impact of the end of Thom. *This is it Marianne. This is really it. It's over—your denial, the charade. IT'S OVER.*

I felt the end of Thom's life. The end of life as I knew it.

I made my way to the car and just sat in the cold, unfit to drive. I tried to pull myself together.

Adjust your thinking, Marianne. You have made it this far pretending that he was going to be okay, but now you KNOW. He is not going to make it.

I think my doctor self was having a heart-to-heart talk with the wife and mother. *Adjust yourself to this new reality.*

The wife and mother replied, *How the heck do you adjust yourself to the impending death of your husband and the father of your children?*

*I don't know. I honestly don't know. But I do know that **we** are the ones who have to pull together on this. We have to be the first ones to know and try to pull it together.*

How can we do this when no one else knows?

Who could I talk to about this? My knee-jerk response was to talk to Thom, but in this case there would be no counseling coming from him.

My doctor head was telling me, *He knows. He is on his third chemotherapy regimen. He has to have an idea that it's not working.*

I had not been to the last few visits with Kert. Maybe they had already spoken about it and I didn't know it. *No, Thom would have said something to me. Maybe he knows and doesn't want to talk about it until after Christmas? That would more like Thom. Considerate.*

I was temporarily sheltered in my car cocoon. I stared out the windshield at the frigid New England landscape. The car rocked when it was hit with a gust of arctic wind, accompanied by a low moaning whine.

Where would my answers come from?

My gaze swept slowly passed the gray overcast skies and the barren ground beneath it as each exhale made small clouds before my face.

Where was the hope? Where would it come from?

I felt as desolate as the scene before me. I was in a time warp where nothing else mattered or even existed. Hopelessness has no time limit.

You might be thinking, like I was, there is nothing out there to offer even a shred of hope. But there they were, like they just showed up. The Trees.

In winter, the trees reveal their structure, their "backbone." You can't see that when the trees are covered with lush greenery—only when they've been stripped bare. They are tough, they are alive, and now they wait in silence, but their core is intact and alive.

The same is true of me, I thought stubbornly. Peeled down to my core, I could discover a strength there I had not recognized or acknowledged before.

I have a backbone too. How else could I have made it this far?

How could I have continued to hold my head up, to go to work, to care for my children, to run my office—not to mention care for Thom and maintain any hope as I watched him lose 80 pounds and become so physically dependent. I may be stripped down, but for damn sure I ain't no weakling.

This conversation calmed me down. My focus slowly returned to the here and now. My plan was to focus on today, regardless of how many todays we had left. One day at a time, just like in AA or any situation that seems overwhelming. Just take each day as it comes. Work through that day. Don't worry about yesterday or tomorrow.

It seemed like the most reasonable plan and it was the only one that presented itself.

*Okay Marianne, if this **is** his last Christmas, what would be an appropriate present for Thom?*

I had no idea, but Caitlin did.

Thom was constantly trying to get Caitlin to take responsibility for her actions and, more importantly, their consequences. Caitlin was thirteen years old and refused to see the connection between what happened to her and her part in creating the results. She would always say, "It was an accident."

Thom's reply was always the same. "An accident is the consequence of an unprepared mind."

There were many ways he would say this same thing. No matter how Caitlin tried to explain how things could just happen accidentally, Thom wouldn't buy it.

If her glasses were broken because she took them off and laid them next to her on the ground, then stood up and stepped on them, it was an accident. Thom would try to point out that if she had put them in a safer place, that "accident" would not have happened.

If her calculator was lost at school (for the third time), Thom would point out that if it was in her backpack that "accidental" loss would not have occurred.

Or if she didn't get her homework in on time because she left something to the last minute and then the computer wouldn't print and there was no time to fix it, Thom would counter with, "It would not have happened if you had prepared for it not to happen."

Granted, the concept is not the easiest to grasp—and definitely not if you are a teenager. Caitlin found these lessons exceedingly frustrating. He must have been teasing her about this for at least six months by the time Christmas came around.

This gave her an idea for a present that she was sure he would love, and she was so excited about it.

She had the t-shirt guy at the mall airbrush a brain on the front of a shirt. Under it, she had printed Thom's favorite phrase:

An Accident Is
the Consequence of
an Unprepared Mind

On Christmas morning, they were both clearly over-the-top pleased with that present. He put it on after opening it, and didn't take that t-shirt off again until the next night.

Thom looked a little surprised, however, when he opened the video camera that I gave him for Christmas. He handled it like it was a satellite bound for the moon and had no clue what he was supposed to do with it.

My intention was to record him and the girls together. I also fantasized about asking him questions that maybe they would like to ask their Dad when they got a little older and he would be gone. Perhaps they could watch the video and still somehow get the sage advice that their Dad would have given them had he still been alive.

It was a great idea, but it never became a reality. I totally misjudged my own energy. Under normal circumstances, learning to operate the camera and then organizing the questions and taking the video would have been easy. But, by Christmas, I was emotionally and physically played out. I looked at the camera's directions and then just handed the camera over to the girls.

They were technically facile. Even though they never looked at the directions, they could operate the camera. They had fun videotaping Thom (a little) and themselves (a lot). Since they had no idea about my agenda, they obviously did not abide by it, but I quickly let go of my disappointment after watching them.

They were just kids enjoying making faces and videoing themselves. We were all in stitches watching them record, play back, record some more, and play back again. They weren't acting like kids with a dying Dad. They were just kids at Christmas.

It was later that night, after Thom and Justine were in bed, that Caitlin and I had some time together. We had been sitting on the hearth by the fire, but then we stood in front of the fire to get its full warmth. We were rubbing shoulders staring into the flames when Caitlin said, "Well, if this is going to be Dad's last Christmas, it sure was a nice one."

Just like that, she said it. She said it as if she was simply exhaling or sighing. So matter-of-fact.

Breathless from the impact of her simple statement, I asked, "Do you really think this is Dad's last Christmas?"

"Yes," she replied softly while still looking into the fire.

"You think that he is not going to make it?" I needed crystalline clarification.

She turned and looked directly in my eyes. "No, Mom. I don't think Dad is going to make it."

She said it like it was a done deal—like she knew it, and had known it for some time.

Looking at her young innocent face, barely fourteen years old, I wondered where she got such wisdom and strength.

Then it hit me. I was not alone. Some other significant person in my life, who does not want to face this reality, also knows the truth.

Thom Waner, husband and father, was going to die. We started to cry as we hugged each other as hard as we could. We confessed how we each knew, but where afraid to talk about it. How we both wanted to be wrong. How we both felt relieved to be able to share with someone else. How we were both scared beyond belief.

After Caitlin went to bed, I stood on the hearth with my back to the fire. I started to think of our immediate future and how this knowledge would change everything. We would have to live differently. And we would have to start now by sharing the news.

But first I had to know. For sure. Right now. I grabbed the phone.

"Kert? It's Marianne. Look, I am sorry to bother you at night, but there is something I need to know and I need to know it now. I want you to tell me the truth."

"Okay," he said tenuously.

"Is Thom going to beat this cancer or not?"

Silence.

Even if he wanted to say something, I didn't give him much of a chance.

"I mean, he has failed three different sets of chemo, and presumably they were his best chances. For a long time—well, from the beginning actually—I felt he wasn't going to make it. But I haven't really spoken to anyone about it because I know hope is a critical element in fighting cancer. I didn't want to be the one to hinder his chances and everyone's hope. But every day I find it harder to be hopeful. Actually, I lost all hope a while back, but I kept quiet about it because I thought everyone else was still hopeful."

I barely paused long enough to breathe.

"So I thought I was better off pretending he was okay, even though it's damn obvious he is not. You know, I thought everyone else was buying into it. But tonight Caitlin said she was sure it was Thom's last Christmas. We talked about it and we are both sure it's his last one. I assume that somewhere deep down inside, Thom knows it's his last one too. So, Kert, if *you* know it's going to be Thom's last Christmas, then we *all* know it. And you know what? We can handle it, but we have to talk about it openly. We have a large family and most of Thom's relatives live in California. They are going to want to spend time with Thom while he is alert enough to enjoy the visit. We will have a lot to do. The worst thing in the world would be for there to be a big mob scene here in the last few weeks of his life and have Thom be too exhausted to enjoy the time with his family."

Finally I ran out of steam. And words.

"Wow, there sure is a lot going on at your house!" he finally said.

"You've got that right. So… Is he going to make it or not?"

"Marianne, let's sit down and talk about this, the three of us, at Thom's office visit this week."

"Well, okay, but I still want to know the answer Kert. I want to know."

"I know. We will talk."

Later that week, the three of us sat in Kert's examining room. Thom sitting in his wheelchair in his winter coat that now looked three sizes too big for him as he was leaning forward on his cane. Kert was on his metal doctor's stool and I was in the only other chair, in the corner of the room. The whole time Kert spoke, he only looked at Thom. The doctor-patient relationship was between those two. I felt like a fly on the wall, completely unnoticed.

They were the two most important men in my life at that time. I observed how they related, more than what they were saying.

Kert was reviewing Thom's progression of his illness. I saw a pale, bald, yet bearded, Thom looking at his doctor from a smaller, more hollow version of the body I have known for sixteen years. Kert looked young and vivacious compared to Thom.

The engagement in their conversation was so sincere, so touching, that it was almost palpable. The concern and love reflected in each face was so real that there was almost a physical presence of light in the room.

Kert was saying, "But the cancer has continued to spread."

I dragged my mind back into the conversation as Kert continued.

"Now it's in the right lung and the spine. By the way, if your back hurts, we can radiate it and knock out a lot of the pain. But most importantly, now you are anemic and we need to give you a couple units of blood and some Epogen to stimulate your bone marrow to make more of its own blood cells. Also, you should take a few weeks off from any further treatments."

"What else is there?" Thom asked.

"There are some new experimental medications. We could enter you into one of the clinical trials."

"What kind of statistics do they have?"

They talked back and forth. I watched.

"So this is where we're headed when you feel up to it," Kert said.

"Right now, I am setting you up for two units of blood. When your blood count is up, we will talk some more. Why don't you go home and think about it?"

Wait! I wanted to scream. *I didn't get my answer!*

Have I been duped by Kert, thinking he would answer my question? Or is there still some shred of hope left out there?

Then I remembered. This was not my visit. I was not the patient. Maybe Thom had to think about all this when his brain had enough blood to actually think halfway normally. I had to give him that opportunity.

A few nights later, in late January, I awoke from a deep sleep at about 1 a.m. to hear water running in the bathroom. My right arm flew over to Thom's side of the bed. Empty.

"Honey?"

No answer. I hopped out of bed and rushed into the bathroom to find Thom urinating into the bathtub.

"Honey? What are you doing?"

I wasn't even sure that what I was seeing was not a dream.

"Well, I couldn't find the bathroom so I decided to pee on this tree over here," he said pointing to thin air.

"What tree?" I asked, scratching my head.

"I got lost and I had 'to go' so bad. This was the best place I could find."

My doctor brain finally woke up. I reached out and touched his arm. It was scorching hot. At least 103 degrees, I assessed.

Okay, he has a high temperature and hallucinations, most likely caused by a pneumonia due to the lung cancer.

"Thom, do you know where you are?"

"No."

"Do you know who I am?"

"Of course I do, honey. Boy, is it cold out here!" Suddenly he started to shake and his teeth started to chatter.

Classic rigors, also supporting my diagnosis of pneumonia.

I grabbed some ibuprofen and an antibiotic from my cabinet. By the time they kicked in, the bed had been shaking like a 4.0 on the Richter scale for about an hour.

The rest of the night was spent holding him, giving him water, and helping him go to the bathroom in the actual toilet. I consoled him by telling him he was alright, which of course he most certainly was not.

Up until this time, I had Dan, an associate Family Doctor of mine, working with me four days a week. He knew the situation with Thom, and probably had a better understanding of it than I did at this point since I was so close to things.

That next work day, I felt like I was dragging 20 lbs of concrete behind me around the office. Twice I had to ask Dan to go over my treatment plans for patients to be sure they were correct. I felt drugged and distant.

I rarely drank coffee, but that day I headed to the coffee shop next door and got a double espresso. On rare occasions, I found caffeine worked for me.

Standing at my work station in the hallway of my office, looking into the bottom of my empty cup, I awaited the usual jolt I desperately needed. Nothing happened. I was still exhausted.

As I continued to stare into the cup, Dan came up to me and asked, "Are you alright?"

His tone of voice let me know that he clearly didn't think so. In that moment, everything in my life shifted. It was the kind of epiphany you don't want.

For twenty years, I had been the best family doctor that I could be. I took great pride in my work. It was a core part of my identity.

But that day, I saw myself as an impaired physician, not by drugs or alcohol, but by sleep deprivation and emotional exhaustion. I was at the end of my rope right there in my office. There was no mental or physical rebound in store for me. Looking into the future, it all seemed dark and murky.

"Dan, this exhaustion is something that espresso can't fix."

Looking into his eyes, I saw my whole professional career come to a halt. In that moment, I knew that he knew it too. Perhaps he had seen it before I did.

I stood there stunned as the tears welled up in my eyes. Before his face went blurry, I could see the empathy in his gaze. He reached out and gave me a long hug.

In the kindest way possible, Dan recommended that I stay home with Thom. He would cover my practice until I was ready to come back to work.

It was a great plan and really the only one that would work. I was spread way too thin. As I left the office that day, I knew that it was time for me to stay home and give Thom my full attention. At the same time, I would miss my office staff, my office family and my patients, all of whom I loved and looked forward to seeing each day.

They would survive well in Dan's hands, but I wasn't too sure how well I would do without them.

The Conversation

"It is the way it is supposed to be." – *Tim Lucid,*
referring to life and death

One morning in January, shortly after I decided to stay home full-time, Thom wanted a shower but was too weak to bathe on his own. We had a walk-in shower that had a long tile bench along the back wall. I thought if I got in there with Thom, I could set him on the seat and easily wash and rinse him. (Yes, cancer does give showering together a whole new meaning.)

We got in without a hitch and all was going well until I finished washing his head and looked at his face, which had gone ashen.

He said he was feeling a little woozy and wanted to sit down. Sitting, he started to look better, so I soaped him up, but he offered no assistance at all.

Suddenly he looked faint and went limp. It was one of those, "Oh, shit!" moments when I realized he was unexpectedly in a pre-faint state. After a quick rinse, I jumped out of the shower, threw a towel on the wheelchair, then stepped back into the shower to grab Thom, but I couldn't lift him. He was too slippery. He had that deer-in-the-headlight look and clearly had no idea how much danger he was in.

"Oh God, give me the strength to lift him," I prayed aloud.

119

As I tried to pull him to a standing position, it felt like he had suction cups holding him to the seat.

How can I get him out of the shower without him falling to the floor and fracturing any number of his cancer-riddled bones? Should I lay him down and call 911?

It was clear I needed help. As I tried to drag him to a standing position, I pleaded with him. "Come on, honey, at least give me some help for God's sake."

His reply was flat, but clear. "You are never going to make it as a geisha, Marianne."

I stood in frozen disbelief, my wet hair dripping in his face. "What?" I exclaimed.

"You are much too rough and too fast."

A geisha? A geisha! I left my medical practice to be called a geisha?

That did it. First I was concerned, then scared half to death, but now I was just plain old pissed off.

"You have got to be freakin' kidding me," I yelled back in exasperation. "What the hell do you think I am doing here? Having a freakin' picnic?"

Perhaps my anger was the answer to my prayers. Totally rip-roaring mad, I pushed my hands under his armpits and clasped them behind his back. I lifted him up, dragged him over the shower's threshold, and plopped him down in the wheelchair.

"See what I mean?" he piped up as he listed to the left.

With that, I wheeled him into the bedroom, picked him up, and threw him into bed just as he passed out.

When I calmed down, I stood at the bedside toweling my hair dry. He was snoring away. I wondered what could have made Thom act so weird and then pass out.

Was he really that weak?

Surely it wasn't the shower or my lack of appropriate "geisha-ness." My eyes landed on the pain pills at the bedside table. We had the total number of pills lined up for the day, but half of them were gone. Somehow he had unintentionally taken most of those in the space of a few hours.

Holy cow, the guy is completely over-medicated. No wonder. He's stoned! Well, I thought, *at least he is not in any pain.*

That's when we started keeping a pain pill log at his bedside. Neither one of us could keep track of time anymore and certainly I couldn't expect the person on the pain pills to be responsible for remembering what he'd taken.

A few days later, once the pneumonia medication was completed, Kert wanted another CT scan—this time, to assess the size of the tumor and determine where to direct the radiation beam to shrink it. Without doing that, the pneumonia would just reoccur.

Now instead of *treating* the cancer, we were into *managing* the cancer so as to reduce its nasty side effects and prolong the quality of Thom's life. Thom dying with fever, chills and hallucinations was not an option I wanted to consider.

As he came out of the scanner, the first thing I noticed were his white knuckles gripping the sides of the slender scanning table. As his torso and then his head came out, I saw the grimace on his face that told me he was hurting, badly. You have to lie perfectly still for at least thirty minutes while they do the scanning, and the cancer in the bones of his spine was causing a lot of pain. Once he was out of the scanner, he was in too much pain to sit up by himself.

"Help me" was all he could squeak out.

As I slowly helped him up, I felt his arms shake like the muscles were twitching from too much exertion. I still wasn't used to thinking of him in such a diminished capacity. After he caught his breath, he looked up at me as if he had just run a marathon.

"Please don't make me get in that thing again," he pleaded. "Promise me that, Marianne. Swear to me that I won't have to do that again. I just can't do it anymore. I think I'd rather die."

I had never heard that "beaten up" quality in his voice before. The sound of it made my stomach knot up.

"Okay, honey," I said. "I promise."

I gathered him in my arms and almost carried him to the car as if he were a mortally wounded soldier being taken from the battlefield. Thank God there weren't many times like this, times when he was beyond his limits of pain endurance.

Surely this was what every person fears about cancer and death—that they will be pushed beyond their tolerance and be in pain beyond their control, that somehow the end of their life will be torture or, worse yet, they will leave their loved ones with memories of them screaming in pain.

Even with the pain pills that he took before we left home, he was there. He was past the absolute limit of what he could take. In the car, as he finally got comfortable, he let out a groan of agony that came from a deep visceral place, a sound that I can recall to this day.

———————————————

Days later, when Thom had rallied from the brutal scanning day, we had "The Conversation," the one I always knew we would have.

It was a quiet morning in February. The girls were at school. Thom and I were relaxing in the bedroom after breakfast. He was leaning back in his recliner and I sat next to him, both of us soaking in the view of the woods.

There was a fresh dusting of snow on the evergreen hemlocks. They looked magical—deep forest-green triangles covered in a glistening coat of white, like princesses dressed up for a winter ball by their fairy godmother.

As I looked at Thom, I noticed the bones in his temples and cheeks, so prominent now. His head was supported by the chair like he couldn't both hold it up and look out at the forest at the same time.

His exhaustion was evident, but his mind had taken flight. He was not seeing the same scene I was.

I waited.

Slowly, he turned to me and his focus returned.

"How are you?" I asked, touching his hand lightly.

"Better now that the pneumonia is gone, but—" He paused. "I'm so tired."

"Anemic-tired?"

He turned and looked at me. I waited for a reply, but he was silent. Most of the time, I could read this mood and even this thoughts, but not now. I felt lost.

Where was he? What was on his mind just then? And now?

He was working up to something. I could tell. We stayed enfolded in each other's gaze for quite some time.

"Honey… I'm dying." he said.

"I know," I whispered.

He looked out the window as if there were some thoughts lingering out there in the forest that would come to his aid, something there to explain or clarify what he wanted to say to me. He looked at me.

"I know where I'm going and it may sound selfish, but I don't want any more chemo."

"Okay." Pause.

"Not even the experimental chemo Kert was talking about?" I asked to be crystal clear.

"No," he answered decisively. "I don't want the end of my life to be spent nauseated and tired. I have a lot to do to get ready."

What he meant by the last statement, I don't know. But I sensed that he knew, and that was all that mattered. He could feel the pull. He wanted to get ready. (*What the hell does that mean?*) We were sitting there, focused solely on each other—two of the best communicators around sitting silent in the most outrageous non-verbal discussion.

I was trying to remain open to him and absorb every meaning. He was sitting forward in his chair propped up by his elbows. His demeanor was imploring me, not only to understand the importance of his decision, but to support him in it.

I slowly answered his unspoken questions. "I understand. This is your life. I want what you want. I will do whatever I can to help you."

"I want to die right here in my own house. In my own bed."

"Okay. You got it."

"No more trips to the hospital or the CT scanner." He looked at me with that one eyebrow raised.

"Yes, I understand. I already figured on that."

He paused for a moment. "I want to say goodbye to everyone. Sarah, my brothers and my Dad. I want everyone to come if they can."

"You've got that too, honey. I'll help you make that all happen."

"Thank you."

He leaned back in his chair and let out a long sigh. He looked out toward the forest again. He was finished. He had come to his conclusion. I knew he wouldn't change his mind. He could make his plans for his ending. Somehow it would be okay. We would make it okay. I knew I would do everything he asked and more. He was going to get everything he wanted at the end. I didn't even have to think about what I would say next.

"No, honey. Thank *you*." I reached out and held his hand.

I wanted to tell him some of the most important things before his mind took flight again. I didn't even know that they were waiting to be said, but now they were urgent. I had to tell him now, while it was still just the two of us, while we were both at the same point, in the same place. While we were in the same mindset. While we had the time alone together.

"You have enriched my life in so many ways. I feel so lucky to have had you in my life for as much time as we've had. I want more, but we both know now that that is not meant to be." I paused to gather my words.

"I have learned more from you than any teacher I have ever had, and I've had some great ones. I understand myself and life in ways I never could have without you. It wasn't always easy living with you, but it was enlightening beyond belief!" We both started to grin.

"I consider it a privilege to take care of you through your dying time, Thom. I pledge to you my very best efforts." I saw his face full of gratitude before it went fuzzy from my tears.

We were connected. When we were married, we said something about standing by each other, come what may. We silently nodded our heads.

We knew. We knew about life. We knew about death. We would go through it together. Together we would face our ending.

After we let the impact of the conversation settle in, we started talking about the end. His ending. How he actually saw himself dying or letting go. "I want it to be peaceful. I *don t* want to go like your mother."

That statement immediately sent me back to the night before she died. We had both been at my mother's bedside for most of the day. She was in a coma. That night, we were sleeping in our motor home parked outside their house. Around 3 a.m. my father was pounding on the door in a panic.

"Marianne, your mother is throwing up and I don't know what to do."

As I came into their bedroom, I could see why my father was in such distress. She had dark blood everywhere and she was gurgling on what was left in her mouth and throat. The doctor in me was thinking about a suction machine like in the hospital, but at her home, no such devices were available. I ran to the kitchen and grabbed the only substitute I could think of—the turkey baster.

While I worked, Thom took my Dad into the kitchen and made them some tea. I cleared the blockage, cleaned her up, changed her clothes, and brushed her teeth, but no matter what I did, I could never completely get rid of the gurgling. It was the most unnerving sound, much worse than fingernails on the blackboard.

Later that morning as my siblings arrived, it drove everyone out of the room. Now I know why they call it the "death rattle." As I sat on my

Dad's bed, next to my Mom's, I became really frustrated. Thom came in and sat in the chair at the foot of her bed.

"I can't get rid of that God-awful noise no matter what I do," I complained.

"Give her some more morphine," he said.

I did. Then I gave her more every five minutes. Twenty minutes later, still no one but Thom and I could stand to be in the room.

"Give her more, Marianne," he said gently.

"I've already doubled the dose the hospice nurse told me to give."

Nodding his head that he understood, he coaxed, "Give her more."

"But if I give her more…" I protested.

Calmly, he replied, "I know. Give her more, honey."

He said, "Look at her. She is about to die. Make her comfortable. Stop the noise so your family can get in here."

Uncomfortable that I might be hastening my own mother's death, I gave her more until it calmed down that awful gurgling noise. It didn't kill her, but did at least allow people to come into the room to say goodbye. She died peacefully hours later.

This is what Thom meant when he said he didn't want to go like my mother had, and I agreed. One experience like that was enough for a lifetime.

He looked at me seriously. "If I do anything weird, I want you to knock me out, okay?"

Trying to picture Thom's body acting in some unnatural, weird, scary way, I wondered what I would do in response. "Okay, honey," I answered somewhat tentatively.

"I mean it," he said emphatically. "I don't want my kids to remember me that way. I don't want their last images of me to be me seizing or throwing up or anything like that."

He didn't need to look that insistently at me. I knew that. I would not let that happen. "I promise you, Thom, if you start acting scary or weird, I'll knock you right out. I promise."

"Thank you," he said softly.

———————————— ✺ ————————————

Our last visit to Kert's office was after Thom's blood count rose to a whopping 10 units of hemoglobin, still below normal, but out of the "sheer exhaustion" range. Kert and Thom were talking about his energy level and how he felt.

There was a brief silence and then Thom asked, "Kert, if I don't take any more chemotherapy, how long would I have?"

Kert knew this was coming. "Well, no one can say for sure how long you have, Thom. I could tell you how long other people have lasted who were in your position."

"Okay." said Thom. "How long would you estimate?"

"I would say about four to six months."

Silence.

"Somehow I was hoping for longer than that," he said looking down and softly tapping his cane on the floor. Then he looked up and added, "I knew I wasn't going to beat this, but somehow I thought maybe it would take a couple of years."

I wanted those years. I wanted them for Thom. I wanted them for Justine and Caitlin and Sarah. I wanted them for me. But I have four to six months. His doctor had just told him that. It was real now in a way that somehow it wasn't before.

Tears streamed silently down my face. I had been holding my breath while I listened to Kert. Whatever shreds of hope there were for Thom were decimated. Seeing him accept the reality of four to six months was like having a guillotine come down. No life left. Now, for the first time, all of us were on the very same page, and not a one of us was happy or hopeful. Not Thom. Not the doctor. Not the wife. Not the mother.

It felt as if someone had reached into my chest and squeezed all the blood out of my heart. It hurt beyond pain. I wanted it to act normally, but my hurting heart just kept on hurting. I had nothing to say. None of us had anything further to say. I wheeled Thom silently back out to the car.

On the way home, there was an oppressive presence in the car that put me in mind of a heavy smog day in Los Angeles, when air doesn't seem to get into or out of your lungs correctly. It's like there isn't enough air to let your lungs fully expand. When you do breath, it hurts. Each breath hurts.

He too had felt the weight of the pretense that he was going to be okay. At this point, however, the weight of reality felt a heck of a lot heavier.

"I have to tell the girls." Thom said this looking through the windshield as if there were several accident victims lying dead along the highway. The set of his jaw and the tone of his voice let me know that he would rather do anything than have to tell his daughters that this was the end. Yet they had to know. And he wanted to tell them himself.

Sitting in the great room on the green velvet couch, he once again had a girl on either side of him.

"We had a long talk with the doctor today," he said slowly and deliberately, as if somehow that could soften the blow. Both their young faces turned up to his expectantly.

"He says my cancer is back. It has not been touched by the three best ways to kill it." He looked at one, then the other.

None of us—Caitlin, Justine or myself—can remember one word that was spoken after that.

Justine and I remember her screaming and accusing us of not being positive enough to believe that her Dad could beat the cancer.

Caitlin hugged her Dad and wept silently until the entire left side of his shirt was wet.

Watching this interchange between my dying husband and his vulnerable daughters was so incredibly painful that although I sat there, I also left. I went away. I went somewhere deep, dark and distant.

Watching that landslide of grief hit my husband and my two daughters, at that moment, in that room, I experienced more pain than I had ever experienced before in my life.

I had to get away. It was like being jet-propelled down a tunnel, a dark tunnel with no light. There was no end in sight. There was no feeling, no sensation of any kind, not even breathing. I was just gone— over the edge of reality.

Life After Hope Is Gone

"If you are breathing, stop complaining it's not like it used to be. Get busy and live." – Glen Allard

Once Thom decided not to take any more chemo and to prepare for death, our life became more focused. There were no more radiation trips, no more chemo mornings, no more chemo shakes, no more nausea, no more blood draws, no more blood transfusions, no more "let's try this," no more "what ifs." Finally, we were all on the same page, the last page of Thom.

It was amazing how free we felt once that decision was made. When hope comes to an end, it's not all bad. Who knew?

The way the medical profession concentrates on "the cure," we tend to think that when no cure is possible, there is nothing left and nowhere to go. The person's hope is decimated and, in some way, so are they. They are left facing the fear of the unknown, unchartered territory. It's scary, like you are running on solid hope and, when that comes to an end, the road ends and the ground beneath your feet disappears and you are still running, right off the end of the cliff, just like the cartoon character Wiley Coyote. There is nowhere to go but flying into thin air and then *splat* you hit the ground and it's over.

But it wasn't like that for us. Actually, we felt a different type of hope and, in some ways, felt more alive than we had in months. The days were alive with Thom-ness. We all felt our spirits elevate. Once his death was accepted, we all started to shift our focus to where:

> "...everything becomes just as it is, just this moment,
> an extraordinary opportunity to be really alive."
> – *Stephen Levine*, from WHO DIES:
> AN INVESTIGATION OF CONSCIOUS LIVING AND CONSCIOUS DYING

We spent minutes, hours and happy times filled with what Thom wanted—what he wanted to do, who he wanted to be with, and what he wanted to eat.

One night, the answer to that question was a complete surprise. "Banana cream pie."

In the sixteen years we were together, he had never had a hankering for it, but this night he did. Sarah and Caitlin tore off on a search and rescue mission for banana cream pie and darned if they didn't find one. I still remember watching him savor each bite. (I think Sarah and Caitlin finished it off.)

The transformation hit all of us at different times and it wasn't accomplished over night. I clearly remember one night when we were all piled into our king-size bed watching a DVD on the laptop computer strategically placed in the middle of the bed. The girls were plastered on either side of Thom as usual. I glanced to my right taking in this idyllic scene of family contentment when all of a sudden a wave of panic hit me.

I thought, *This is ridiculous! We are watching a **movie** and Thom is dying! We should be **doing** something.*

But there was Thom beaming, contented snuggling with his girls, and I thought, *What else **should** we be doing? What was better than this? Surely we can't keep talking and planning for death all day and night. Besides he isn't dead yet! There is still a lot of time for us to enjoy him.* So I willed the emotional tsunami back out to sea.

Honestly, I don't remember the movie at all, but I do remember soaking up that luscious quality time of all of us being together.

Thom knew what he wanted and wasn't afraid to ask for it. He was becoming comfortable with the idea of dying. There was no fear, no freaking out, his attitude set the mood for everyone.

Most days now, he and I meditated together in the afternoon lying on our bed. It was a calming and comforting time. There was only this one time that he questioned himself. At the end of our meditating, he turned to me, his eyes wide. "Do you think I have done *enough* good in my life?"

Did he make enough good choices in his life? Did he do good enough to get where he was going? Did he do his family proud?

I thought of all the patients I had referred to him, some of them extremely difficult. So many came back to me thanking me for recommending Thom and telling me how significantly improved their lives were because of the work they did with him. I had absolutely no doubt in my mind as to the answer to his question, but I could see that there was doubt in his.

"Thom, I imagine anyone who is in your position would ask a question like that. Or at least they should. In your case, there is no doubt. I have witnessed the powerful impact you have had, the many improvements you have helped bring about in so many patients that I know personally." I named off about ten people right off the top of my head. "Yes, honey, I do think you did a tremendous amount of good for a significant number of people. In many cases, I don't know anyone who could have done as much as you did."

He looked so relieved. "Oh, good." was all he said as he closed his eyes.

So many patients at this same stage of their lives have shared their regrets. Think about it. Your life is coming to an end. You look back and reflect on what you have done, how you made an impact, and what goodness you may take forward. No matter the religious persuasion, everyone takes stock at the end if they have time. The good is so much easier to focus on, but there is no denying the regrets.

Ric told me that once Thom knew he was dying, he started planning for his death as if he were planning an important event. (Who does this? Look at all the time devoted to a birth, a wedding or a graduation. Maybe we should all do a lot more planning on the other end.)

Lots of energy was directed into his death plan. He couldn't tell me the specifics because only Thom knew what they were, but Ric said that the idea was like moving aside the veils of everyday reality to see more clearly into the core of the consciousness beyond. Thom got better and better at bridging the two worlds.

The transformation was "from earth to the clouds," as Ric put it. Thom communicated with or to whatever spiritual beings he thought were there on the other side of this life. I guess when Thom finally did go over and stay there, the path would be well worn and comfortable.

Ric continued his weekly visits every Tuesday. Often after he left, Thom would have an aura of unbelievable peace, almost rapturous.

Gail, our housekeeper, and I were intensely curious about what went on in those meetings. She showed up every Tuesday in her frizzy black/gray hair in her baggy t-shirt over her cropped tights and beat up tennis shoes with her vacuum in tow.

Earlier in Thom's illness, when I would come home from work, she would fill me in on what happened that day. Usually the report was the same: they burned sage, then sometimes it was quiet and sometimes they beat their drums. But one Tuesday at the end of a long string of Tuesdays, Gail was all electrified when I got home.

"There were spirits all over the place!" she said as she waved her polishing rag over her head like a lasso before attacking the kitchen table in a rubbing frenzy. "They filled up that great room in there." She jerked her head toward the other room so as not to interrupt her polishing. "And they stayed for a good long while too. Even after Ric left."

134

I stepped into the great room to see if there was any remnant or lingering feeling of something spiritual there that I could see or feel. Nothing.

"Could you see them, Gail?"

"Nope. But I sure could feel them. Happy full spirits here for Thom's sake. They are waiting for him, Marianne. They are going to greet him on the other side." She stated that matter-of-factly while madly polishing every horizontal surface she could find. She was on to the piano now. "Yup, there are always some of them here when Ric is here, but today was a red letter day, I tell yah." She was almost short of breath.

"Did they do anything different in there today?"

"Who knows. Same ol' smelly sage and the usual amount of drum beating and singing, but whatever they did, they sure did have a lot of spiritual company."

I was jealous. I wanted to be able to feel all those spiritual beings too. I do believe that they were here and was happy for that, but darn it, I wanted to be in on it too. I wanted the reassurance that there was someone or something on the other side of this life and that they would be there for Thom. If there was no cure and no miracle for him here, I wanted some feeling that what he was working toward was real.

I never did see or feel any spiritual beings though. Probably I was too stressed. I had to go it on my own beliefs and faith. I guess I always will until it's my turn, but I did get to experience the drumming.

When Thom became too weak to drum and chant, he and Ric invited the girls and me to join them. They all sat cross-legged on the floor in the bedroom in front of the slider that looked out over the forest, holding the drum in one hand and the beater in the other on their laps. I sat cross-legged on the bed next to Thom so he could put his hand on my back and at least feel the vibrations.

Ric would start chanting, and we quickly learned a call and response pattern. Really, there is no wrong way to do it. You just beat your drum to the song. The sound ricocheted around the room and wound up in your chest, like the feeling you get standing on the sidewalk when a large marching band parades by.

The drumming itself might be easy, but there is a whole lot more to that drumming than you might think. The range of emotions that can be communicated with the tempo and strength of the beating is huge. Each drum sounds different too. With several drums beating at the same time, the experience is completely different. Combine that with the chanting and then add in each person with a different chant and something really powerful happens. Your whole body feels like it's humming.

That first time, there was so much drumming force coming out of my body that my hands blistered. I wanted every one of those spirits to know that Thom was coming—for them to know that someone special was preparing to come over, and for them to make a way for him—to help him transition—to know that he was loved and would be greatly missed.

I never asked the girls what their experience with the drumming was like for them. It doesn't matter. I think it was intensely personal and it had its own meaning for each of us. When you have an experience like that there is no comparison. It just is.

Dying Man's Power

"I didn't get cheated. I had a great run. I want that on my tombstone: Live, Love, Laugh." – Vincent McCauley

Quite the opposite of what you might think, a dying man has a lot of power. As Thom became more physically diminished, his effect on people became greater. A good example was the conversation we had with his stepdad, John. After John heard that Thom was dying, he called the house. I answered the phone.

"Marianne, I know he wants me to come out to see him, but I can't come. My health is really poor. I have so much wrong with me now. The diabetes has affected my eyesight and kidneys. My bowels too give me constant pain. I really don't think I could make the trip all the way to Connecticut from California."

I was disappointed because I knew how important he was to Thom in his formative years. He was there every day for a major part of Thom's growing up. They had a good relationship and an obvious affection for each other.

"I am really sorry to hear that, Dad. I wish you could make it too."

I walked into the bedroom with the phone. I was not going to carry on conversations behind Thom's back, nor was I going to let John off easy either.

"Okay Dad. Here is Thom. You can talk to him yourself." I handed the phone over to Thom, not giving John a chance to say "No."

"Hi, Dad." Pause.

"Yes, well, I'm dying." Pause.

"I want you to come out here so I can say goodbye to you." Pause.

"Okay, good. I'll give you back to Marianne. She'll give you the phone number of someone who can pick you up at the airport."

Smiling, he handed the phone to me. With my hand over the phone, I mouthed to Thom, "He's coming?" He nodded his head yes.

In the snap of a finger, John did a 180 just because Thom asked him to. When a dying man asks you to do something for him, it's pretty damn near impossible to refuse.

John came and visited for two days. It was just enough time for them to reminisce and say their farewells. There was an obvious sadness when he left, but more importantly there was a feeling of contentment. The overriding feel was, "Glad to have shared some of my life journey with you, and thanks for being there." A bittersweet experience that was repeated many times with others who came.

Thom's meditation was a given by now and I tried not to interrupt him during that time. He was going into the afterlife with a clean slate. It was a conscious predilection as if he had a checklist in his head: Things I Want to Do or Think About Before I Die. He was checking them off one by one. He was wrapping up the loose ends of his life.

One quiet afternoon, I was reading next to him as he meditated. Then I felt his eyes on me, waiting for me to look at him. *How powerful they could be.* I turned and looked at him expectantly.

"Marianne?"

"Yeah, honey?"

"There is one more important thing I want you to do for me."

Wanting to please him, I answered, "Sure, honey. Anything. You know that. What is it?"

"I want you to make up with your sister before I die." He said it so matter-of-factly, like he was asking for me to get him a piece of toast or something. And reconciling with my sister was not nearly so simple.

"Really?!"

"Yes," he said simply.

My mind began racing with thoughts of what that would mean. Still shocked, I looked over at him, only to see him lying there with his eyes closed. *He's resting now and I am being swept downstream in a torrent of emotions?*

I stared at him in disbelief. *So now he was my spiritual secret keeper?* But he knew my failings. He knew what I needed to do to progress spiritually. In a flash, I knew he was right, but I was still resisting.

"It's about time," he added, talking slowly and deliberately as if this had been a well thought out plan.

How could I be angry with him, because, first off, I knew he was right. Secondly, the guy was dying and he was requesting this of me— not lecturing, not pleading, simply requesting.

"There will never be a better time to do it. I mean, if you don't do it now while I am dying, when will you do it?" He paused between each thought he delivered while he laid there with his eyes closed.

"Now is the time.

"She is your only sister.

"You need her.

"Call her."

He said no more and clearly was finished with what he wanted to say about me and my sister.

"I'll think about it," I said.

I realized I was full of it. Of course I was going to do it. He was right. It was time to let go of the one grudge that I'd kept for years.

All sibling relationships have their history. My sister, Regina, and I surely had ours. Being the only two girls with four brothers, it was inevitable that our mother would compare us. Regina was nine years younger than me. I was not living at home, and I was ignorant of what my mother said to my sister in my absence. All the "Why don't you do this like Marianne" or "Your sister did this, so why don't you do that too?" etc.

Over the years, the built-up resentments had a disastrous result on our relationship. In addition, when I would come home from college or medical school, my mother would get all excited and energized. She would plan family parties or special shopping trips. She would brag to her friends about how proud she was of her oldest daughter. She put updates of my accomplishments in the local paper.

I think there are ways a parent can brag about one child without the others feeling negatively affected, but my Mom didn't know how to do that. Regina must have had "a craw full" of my praises.

We had dozens of family pictures with everyone smiling, but Regina. Sometimes she would not look at the camera or wouldn't smile or would put on a defiant look. When I asked my Mom what was the matter with Regina, she would reply that Regina was a sourpuss.

Since she wouldn't talk to me, I simply accepted that she was an angry kid. I just never knew why.

When she got out of college, we struggled to get a healthy relationship going. We pieced the whole puzzle together by talking for hours and hours in the hot tub.

We lived together for a few years. Then we went through the death of my fiancé, her marriage to a guy who I thought was a jerk, her divorce (yeah, I was right—but I wish I wasn't), my marriage to Thom, and the birth of our respective daughters. Eighteen years of triumphs and tribulations.

When we left California, it pushed Regina over the edge. She felt lonely and abandoned and angry with me, again.

The odd thing was that, despite the fact that I was the one who moved back to New England with the whole family, I felt more alone, abandoned and displaced than she did—or at least as much.

There were lots of reasons why moving "back home" felt like I had moved to another planet. Most of it had to do with dealing with what I thought were dysfunctional family systems that hadn't changed in the 25 years since I had left. Dealing with a few of my brothers and their behavior toward me and Thom was a rude awakening.

Even worse, it came at a time when Thom was not emotionally available to me. (This was when he was drinking heavily, but I didn't know it.) I reached out to Regina for a lifeline. I needed some grounding, a reality check, and significant emotional support. She shut me down. She told me in no uncertain terms that she did not want to hear about my problems, especially with our family members. Period. I was on my own.

There haven't been many times in my life when I've been that emotionally needy. Besides which, I am a pretty proud person. Asking her for help and being turned down hurt. It hurt big time…

I decided, *If after all we've been through, you don't want to hear my pain because you are uncomfortable hearing something negative about your siblings, well then you can just go to hell! And you're a goddamn therapist?*

My heart went to war. I walled off the sister part of my life and pretended I didn't have a sister. I justified my feelings by making her out to be the ogre. If I couldn't get understanding, I didn't want a relationship. It was that simple. I stopped calling. I stopped talking. Oh I was polite, but that was as far as I went. After a few years, I stopped expecting her to ask what was wrong.

Thom knew all this, but more importantly he knew two key things about feelings. One is that under all anger is hurt. The other is that holding a grudge against someone (especially someone you love) is a powerfully negative thing.

I must say that the energy expended in working on a relationship is a whole lot better than the energy spent on righteous anger. I knew that all along, but I guess I thought it was easier to be angry than hurt.

As I write this now, I'm thinking this sounds awfully petty. But what can I say? It is the truth. We all can be pretty petty with our families sometimes. The point is that at some point we have to let it go. *Maybe this is the time for me to let go. If I don't do it now and I didn't do it when our mom died, when would I?*

When Regina called me and was crying about how upset she was that Thom was dying, I saw my opportunity. She kept saying that she wanted to do something to make things easier for me, but she was so far away that she couldn't help. So I opened my calendar and saw a week where I had no one penciled in to help me care for Thom.

"Well, I could use some help the third week of February." I said this more like a challenge than a sincere opening for her to help. I never really expected her to be able to come. She surprised me by saying without hesitation, "I'll be there."

She came and she did whatever Thom or I asked of her. She sat quietly reading at the foot of his bed while I would run into work for a few hours. She also got a chance to spend time with the girls, which they all enjoyed. All the thoughtful things did not go unnoticed. She sincerely wanted to do something for me and Thom and the girls.

The efforts she put forth were what tipped the balance for me to let go of my anger and hurt. The walls came down that were a barrier to love and understanding. It was one of the smarter things I have done in my life because now I see how much love and life with my sister I would have missed. Now I am on the watch for righteous anger, because I know how easily it can steal your heart.

Regina had only been here a few days before she got a firsthand experience of some of what I'd been dealing with in terms of our family.

The three of us were in the bedroom, she sat in a chair at the foot of the bed, the sun slanted across her shoulder. Thom was lying on his left side facing me, and I was propped up next to him. It was one of those lazy easy days where conversations wander almost on their own. Then there was a knock on the front door.

Stepping out of the bedroom, I was surprised to see my brother, Shawn, through the door's large glass window. He was dressed in his usual black pants and shirt, his black leather jacket and his black beret. Having it pulled over his right ear made the pierced gold cross in his left ear all the more outstanding.

These parts of his outfit have been his signature fashion statements for as long as I can remember. His long, salt and pepper, thinning hair curled behind his ear and down to his shoulders.

It must have been pretty difficult for Shawn to come, because the smell of alcohol preceded him into the room. He sat uncomfortably to the left of Regina. Initially, he sat quietly while we chatted, but his eyes were darting around the room from face to face. I doubt he heard the conversation over his own internal dialogue because suddenly he stood up and started to yell at the floor as if he was in an argument.

"It's not right, man. This wasn't supposed to happen. Not like this. Not this way." He began pacing like those large cats at the zoo, the ones pissed off because they are in those tiny cages. "We were supposed to cook together. We were supposed to have more time together."

He was looking at Thom, but he was not seeing the frail body lying there. He was seeing his brother-in-law with whom he clearly wanted a better relationship, and his potential friendship was eroding before his eyes. His idea of a future with Thom was being stolen by cancer.

"This is fucked up, man. It's not right." He emphatically pointed to the floor to underscore how upset he was.

Now Regina and Thom and I were also upset. It felt as if we were in a rocketship breaking earth's gravity, plastered back in our seats by its tremendous force, able to see and possibly comprehend, but unable to move or speak.

Normally, at work, any one of us would know how to deal with a patient venting their anger. But an emotional outburst in our bedroom left two therapists and a family doctor frozen like kids in a game of Red Light. Defenseless, we had left our tools at the office.

Honestly, I don't remember what Regina and I said to disarm our angry brother. He was possibly just getting in touch with the immensity of his loss. There was no resolution. He left angry.

Thom looked as if he had just taken a beating. He said nothing, but the look he gave me said it all. Distressed—and so vulnerable.

"Honey, I am so sorry about this. It never occurred to me that Shawn would act out like this, indulge his anger in front of a dying man."

Thom was listening but still seemed to be reeling from the whole experience.

"In some way it's a screwed up compliment. He obviously wanted a healthier relationship with you. Now he knows he can't have it. I guess it's his way of grieving the loss of your relationship. I'm sorry, honey. But please try to forgive him—he's been drinking."

"It's okay. I understand him," he said resolutely, "but please, don't let him in here again."

I promised. I didn't really know how I would make that happen, but I knew that I would to keep Thom from any undue stress. Thankfully, Shawn never came back.

By the time Regina had to leave, we had worked out our whole mess. She was surprised that I was angry about her lack of support. I was equally surprised that she didn't realize how important she was to me. I guess because she was the younger sister and I had so often been the one who helped her, she just didn't see it when I needed her.

Obviously, Thom was right on every count. It sure felt great to have my sister back in my life. I was glad he asked me to make up with Regina and I'm equally glad I was smart enough to do it. Getting good advice is important, but acting on takes a whole other level of understanding and commitment.

The In-Laws

"The most loving thing is that we were all there for Dad when he died."
— *E. Schultz*

It took Thom's brother, Steve, about five days to get here by train from San Diego. He has that fear of flying thing. Our friend, Allen, picked him up at the train station in New Haven. He was going to stay a few weeks, but it wound up being a month.

You could tell he and Thom were brothers even though they looked nothing alike. They grew up in the same house: same mother, different fathers. They cooked the same way and ate the same things and told stories about each other that had us all laughing until our sides ached.

Having Steve here shopping, cooking and teasing the girls was almost like having the old Thom back. Steve and I went to Caitlin's Christmas school concert when she was a freshman. She was in an *a cappella* group that had a poor performance that night. (She later directed them and completely turned it into a great group.) The important thing is that he went there in Thom's stead, and Caitlin and I both appreciated it.

Steve, of course, went right to Villarina's and bought things like black and green olives, specialty cold cuts and other finger foods to "keep Thom as good as possible, for as long as possible." He cooked

145

fish, steak, baked potatoes and whatever he thought Thom would like. Thank God, I got a break from the cooking.

Steve sustained us all. His food, his stories, his almost non-stop banter was just what we all needed. He teased the girls and buoyed us along in the dead of winter.

Surprisingly, I never saw him smoking while he was here. Naively, I thought he had given it up. When I mentioned it to the girls, they said they would see him outside the back door smoking and also oftentimes crying.

They noticed when he came in, his eyes would be all puffy and red. I never even recognized it—so much for my powers of observation back then.

Steve and Thom had many conversations in the bedroom. They had their issues growing up like most of us do, some sibling rivalry between #1 son and #2 son, very similar to the issues my sister and I had.

Exactly what went on in their conversations, I'll never know. But one thing was clear: a loving connection was obvious. This I knew by the change that evolved in the way they related to each other.

Initially, conversation was strained and a little nervous, like two old friends meeting up after a long separation. But they found their common ground and, over time, the comfort and laughter was evident, despite the heaviness that brought about the visit.

These old reunited friends had a very difficult time parting for their last time. The girls and I were crying to see him go. Steve was red-eyed and choked up when he left the bedroom. I could feel his pain. He was losing his big brother and I was losing not only a brother-in-law, but a great support person. *Would we ever see him again?*

As with Steve, Thom and his other brother, John, also didn't look like brothers. John, a blue-eyed blond, had the same father, Howard, and a different mother, Jean. Not only did they grow up in different households, but often on different continents. After Howard and Jean were married they moved to South America and later to England.

There weren't many opportunities for brotherly bonding, but I clearly remember the time when they became a lot closer.

John lived in Huntington Beach and had several roommates all about 25 to 30 years old. Apparently there was some discussion among them before they placed a 911 call to Thom. They were worried about John. He was drunk every night. Falling down drunk or rather, not getting up, kind of drunk. They didn't know what to do. Could Thom help?

How someone can polish off a quart of vodka each night and still show up for work the next day is beyond me. People today may think of an alcoholic as some homeless dirty person, unshaven, drinking out of a paper bag, and sleeping under a park bench somewhere. That is *not* today's drunk. (Perhaps that's how the modern-day alcoholic convinces himself that he is not a "real alcoholic.")

Thom drove down to the beach that night and got the story from their point of view. After hours of conversation with John, Thom convinced him to stop drinking and encouraged him to join Alcoholics Anonymous.

That was when John started to become more a part of our lives. Not only did he come to visit more, but when he was with us he was fully present, not dulled by alcohol. This sober John was a whole lot more fun to be around too. He engaged in conversations and laughed about ten times more than when he was drinking. Later on he taught my daughters things he knew about computers, photography and printing. He never would have been able to do that if he wasn't sober.

For sure, John was one of the important people Thom wanted here at his ending. I knew little of their sibling issues, but those are what push us apart and then pull us together into a new understanding. If we are lucky, we acknowledge the issues and deal with them.

Since I was not in the bedroom when they spent a lot of time together, I don't know how it went. Perhaps it wasn't even mentioned.

But since it wasn't like Thom to hold back from his family in the past, I assumed he didn't hold back from John then either. I imagined snippets of conversation:

"You forgot about me when you went to school."

"Remember how you let me take the blame when you did…"

"I am sorry now that I didn't do things differently then."

"You matter to me. You always did, but I didn't show it enough."

My ideas could be way off. Anything could have happened. There might have been accusations flung in every direction. Yet what came out of that room was a joyous feeling, the kind you get when you step outside after a thunderstorm. A fresh clean smell and calm kind of feeling.

This wasn't the case with all visitors, but definitely was true for the brothers. A harmony among the players, orchestrated by Thom, and the whole symphony playing their hearts out in their own way. If there could be a color attached to this feeling, it would be sparkling white.

Howard, Thom's father, could hardly wait for the okay from his hip surgeon after his fracture was repaired, so he could travel from California to see Thom. He needed help and John traveled with their Dad back and forth. Our friend, Allen, owns an airport limo service and was right there at the gate with a wheelchair for Dad.

When they arrived here, Allen and John literally lifted Dad across our large uneven granite entryway and right into the atrium. He stood there shaking like a baby bird who landed outside the nest for the first time.

How did he get so shrunken and frail? Despite being shorter and more stooped over than his last visit, he still had those sparkly blue, Paul Newman eyes. They twinkled under that full head of thick brown-gray hair. They searched the room as he approached me for a hello kiss.

"Do you want to go see him now, Dad?"

"Yes, I do."

148

As I led the way into the room, I heard the tinny clink of the walker each time he set it down. Clink. Take a few steps. Pick it up. Move it forward. Clink. Take a few steps. Until he was all the way over to Thom.

I will never forget how they sized each other up. Thom looking at his frail father after a long and exhausting trip, not to mention the recent operation. Dad was looking at his frail, bald son who could not even get out of bed to greet him.

Despite the shock and sadness evident on each face, the overriding emotion was, "Thank God I am alive to see you."

After getting Dad seated, I backed right out of the room.

Later, after serving everyone lunch, both Thom and Dad were ready for a nap. Dad was in the recliner in the sunny part of the great room. His turquoise eyes sparkled and he wore a smirky grin as he thanked me for lunch. It was funny how he didn't even have a receding hair line, just hair that was thick and full like Thom's when he had hair.

Aside from the eye color, their resemblance was striking. As I tucked him in under a blanket with a cup of coffee, I thought about how he had buried his wife three years earlier and seventeen years before that he had buried his daughter. Now Thom. How did he do it?

He sighed deeply, then reached into his bag and brought out his pipe and proceeded to fill it with tobacco, then lit it. I was stunned. No one, and I do mean no one, had or has since smoked inside this house.

If he had recalled, he would have remembered that the previous times he was here, he had to smoke outside on the porch.

I stood there looking at him finally getting comfortable for the first time of his visit. I swallowed and turned to him and said, "I'll get you an ash tray."

About then, Caitlin and Justine came into the kitchen and were aghast at seeing a cardinal rule being broken as they looked at the white curlicues of smoke all about their grandfather's head inside our house. They called me aside in the kitchen.

"Mom! You let Grandpa smoke in the house?" they quietly admonished me.

"Yes, I did."

"How could you?" they protested in unison.

"How could I not? Look at him. Do you think I am really going to ask that feeble old man who is visiting his dying son to go outside to smoke in the middle of winter?"

They looked across the kitchen into the great room under the small cloud of smoke to their Grandpa and their mutinous stance soften.

"Do you think the two of you could put up with it for a few days?" I requested.

"Sure, Mom." Caitlin answered softly, Justine then reluctantly agreed.

Dad and Thom really enjoyed each other during that last visit. Despite all the hard parts, they were so glad to have pulled it off. Maybe they had an unspoken agreement that being together was the most important thing in the world, now more than ever.

The logistics of getting Dad back to California took all of our concentration. By the time he was on his way up the driveway and I went back in to Thom, he was fast asleep. Exhausting work, this goodbying.

It wasn't long after my brother Shawn's visit that Thom's Aunt Marge called. She too wanted to come see Thom. It was funny how, in the last four years, we could never get her out here. On the phone, she was telling Thom that he needed to be more positive and he should be meditating on his immune system attacking the cancer. She went on to tell him to do all the things that he had been doing for months, the same things that never worked.

What she didn't understand was that the time for this approach was long gone. He was trying to tell her this, but somehow she just couldn't take it in. He was even past the acceptance phase and was now into the goodbye phase. She was giving him outdated advise. She may have been in the right book, but she was far from being on the right page.

To hear someone you care for espousing poorly timed advise is distressing. It is not really the dying person's responsibility to update everyone as to where they are. Maybe it was mine, but I didn't know that, nor did I have the energy. I thought if they didn't get it, maybe they just weren't going to. To top it off, Thom had been there when Marge's husband was dying. Presumably, she should have been more in tune to what was going on with Thom now.

"Marianne," Thom said defeatedly, "I want to see everyone who wants to come, but I don't have the energy to deal with other people's feelings and agendas. I need to have anyone who comes here support my decision."

I flashed back to Shawn's visit and vowed to protect Thom from anyone who could possibly steal his waning energy. No more trying to help people come to terms with Thom's dying.

After considering this, I said to Thom, "I don't think we can afford to go through any more of those episodes. If Aunt Marge didn't matter, it would be a lot easier to talk her out of it. Maybe we should tell her not to come?"

"But I can't do that," he complained.

"I know that, honey, but I can." So I did. I turned her down. It wasn't easy and it wasn't pretty. It surely hurt her feelings. Even now when I think about it I feel sad for Marge and for me, but not for Thom. He had so little energy. I had to protect that—even from family.

Bonnie and Thom had a bond. The easy way they communicated and the relaxed form of their bodies when they spoke and laughed made it obvious. It was like there was some inside joke going on that only the two of them got. They could slip easily between teasing and cajoling each other, right in to something heavy. Old friends, like an old comfortable coat, slipped on in a comforting and expected fashion.

Theirs was a trust and mutual understanding built by hours of heartfelt conversation. A meeting of like minds. Bonnie, the congregational minister, and Thom, the death and dying therapist.

Long before he couldn't get out of the house anymore, he had asked Bonnie to be the minister for his funeral service. Of course she agreed.

Often, she visited at the house to see how her friend, Thom, was doing. Sometimes she stayed for one of our bedroom dinners.

I clearly remember one evening when it was just the three of us. I made New York strip steaks and twice-baked potatoes, Thom's favorite, and I had it down perfectly. In postprandial bliss, we were kicking back and having a rousing discussion on spirituality. It got kicked off by a question I put to Bonnie.

Did she have any suggestions on how I could explain to my father that my lifelong commitment to medicine *was* a spiritual commitment. My father was convinced that I wasn't religious anymore since I didn't go to church on Sunday.

The three of us bantered ideas back and forth about our thoughts of organized religion verses spirituality. Somehow it brought us back to our coming of age back in the late sixties. All three of us were activists and feminists back then, and now all these years later, and under these unusual circumstances, we were joined by significant career and life choices that even now, were true to our beliefs back then. It almost seemed like we were back in the dorm having one of those late night philosophical discussions. Pretty soon we were telling stories of college days and laughing till our full bellies were sore.

Those visits were in stark contrast to the visit we had when she came as "Bonnie the Minster." Looking back now, I am not sure whether this visit was a spontaneous happening or a behind the scenes neatly orchestrated event. Either way it was clear that this visit was a difficult one for her.

This conversation we were about to have, I am sure she has had many times with many families, but not with her friend. And not with Thom, even though he had requested it.

This visit came at a time when Thom was still able to walk around inside the house. We all gathered around on the couches in the great room. Bonnie was on the green couch and Thom was in the rocker. Across from them, I sat on the purple couch.

"I would like the girls, as well as Marianne, to sit and talk about this with us also," he said to Bonnie. We called the girls to join in.

Bonnie got permission to have the service in the Congregational Church in the small church in our town. This church was where the Friday night AA meetings were held. It felt very homey and, since Thom was baptized a Congregationalist, it seemed like the right place.

Bonnie started out, "Thom and I were talking about his church service. The one we will have for him after he dies. He has some ideas and maybe you do too." No one said anything, not so much from shock, as from thinking what would be included in a service like that for Thom.

"This is your service, Thom, what do you want?" she asked.

Thom thought about it for a minute. "I know what I don't want. I don't want sadness," he said slowly.

"Okay," said Bonnie. "It could be a celebration of your life."

"That's it. That's what I want," responded Thom with enthusiasm. "Keep it upbeat. And…" he looked directly at Bonnie, "I don't want a lot of psalm reading or a lot of preaching either."

This started a discussion about what each of us thought made a good funeral service and most especially what we hated that we had sat through in the past. Bonnie was wondering if we took out all the things Thom didn't want, what would we put in?

Thom had some definite ideas, "I want my girls to be able to say something, if they want to," he said looking at the girls and they were shaking their heads in agreement. Then he looked at me, "And you too, Marianne. But promise me you won't go on and on."

"Well, thanks a lot!" I chided indignantly. "What makes you think I am going to go on and on?"

"Honey," he said using those riveting eyes of his, "I know you."

"Well, I am not going to go on and on, so you can relax." I said folding my arms across my chest.

"Okay. Good." He said.

"I want music." He added. "The kind where everyone sings together."

Another discussion about music, different types of songs. We are a musically oriented family so we each started throwing out different ideas.

Bonnie rejected, "I Can't Get No Satisfaction" by the Rolling Stones as a recessional, even though we all loved that idea. I asked Bonnie if the a cappella group, Femina Melodia, the one she sang in, would consider singing a song or two. She thought they would.

Half the women in the group played African drums. After all the drumming that had gone on here at home, drumming seemed a natural for Thom's church service. Would they do that too? She would ask.

Thinking about who would be at the service, I thought there may be some of Justine's friends and classmates. Having dealt with many children and adults who have a fear of dying and especially dying in their sleep, I wanted to make sure that Bonnie didn't say anything associating going to sleep with death. She was totally clear about that. She knew about that too.

As we all sat quietly thinking, Thom said, "That's it. That's all I need. Keep it simple. At the end, let anyone who wants to tell a story, tell it."

Then he looked at me and added, "Afterward, feed everyone."

"Got it," I answered.

I knew all I had to do was put Sue from Villarina's on the alert and they would do a great job.

Months before, one of my patient's sent me a note stating that she would do whatever I needed. She included her home number and said she wouldn't bug me with a call, but to call her when the need arose. I took Dottie up on her offer. Would she coordinate with Villarina's to set up the things needed in the church after the memorial service?

"I'd be glad to," she instantly replied.

I considered it done.

It seemed like planning the funeral was just another thing that Thom thought of and could take care of before he died. Having him participate in the planning of the memorial service somehow seemed natural. I was glad we did it while he was able to get up and walk around because it seemed far from eminent. But one look at Bonnie in the beginning of our discussion, with her voice cracking and her eyes all teared up, let me know how hard it was for her. She no doubt had overseen hundreds of these services, but visualizing herself officially there for her friend was not easy. And that is putting it mildly.

More Visitors

"My passport is in order." – Fred Martin,
when facing his own death.

"Jim, you have to come see Thom," I said emphatically. Jim was our chiropractor and friend, and I was at his office for a visit. Besides working out the kinks in my neck, our visits always included a quick spiritual checkup. The discussions had recently become centered around Thom's progress—or decline, depending on how you looked at it. He knew Thom was in the last stages of dying at home.

"You won't believe what he looks like now," I added excitedly. He looked at me oddly. "Oh, I don't mean physically. Of course, he is a shadow of his former self. He is totally exuding spirituality. I know you're someone who can really appreciate what's going on with him, but you have to see it to believe it. And Jim," I added softly, "he is pretty close to the end, so don't wait too long."

Jim came and brought his massage table. He massaged Thom, which made him more comfortable. Afterward, Jim and Thom spent a fair amount of time talking. Jim came back a few more times too. They seemed to be mutually beneficial visits.

Observing the ending of Thom's spiritual transformation was a great treat for me. Even as he became weaker and smaller, his frail body often in pain, he grew to be a spiritual giant.

In Native American spirituality, the circle that was Thom was becoming significantly larger day by day. It now took up the whole room that he was in. In intangible ways, you could see it or feel it. It was as if he was a song in perfect harmony. Being around him felt like being bathed in positive, unconditional regard. Plain and simple—he was resonating love.

When he spoke, it came from a place of deep peace and understanding. People wanted to hear what Thom had to say. Whatever he was saying was more important to them now because they could feel his connectedness to some inner truth. Thom was plugged into goodness and they wanted a piece of it.

This is how I explained the experience to my friend. Cancer scrubbed you totally clean, like some big, spiritual loofah has scrubbed you down to the bare essentials. All the external trappings of our lives and how we had presented ourselves each day to the world were scrubbed right off. What really mattered most was what's left—a bright, shiny, clean and radiating love, and sharing the moment with people who matter, being completely engaged with them.

There is a connectedness that flows back and forth that accentuates the absolutely best part of being human. It's a natural high that defies description. Once you have experienced this reality, it changes you for the better. It is like the aching and searching that leads a soul through life has found what it always wanted—itself. It is a contentment that says, "I have come full circle. I am now complete. I need nothing more, only this."

When you stay in this mindset, it rubs off on the people around you. You don't realize how much it has changed you nor how obviously changed you appear. Now even more people were drawn to Thom. Our house had been a quiet place at the end of a dead-end. Now it felt like Grand Central Spiritual Station.

As the word got around that Thom was failing, more people called and came by. It got to the point that before I came into the bedroom from taking a shower in my own bathroom, I had to knock on the door between the bathroom and the bedroom because someone might have come in to visit Thom while I was in the shower.

For sure, there was no more trotting naked through the bedroom to the closet. It was such a simple, but significant, difference in my own private routine. It epitomized the degree of change that had occurred in our everyday life.

So many people came that I had to go to the office and get Thom's abandoned schedule book so we could keep everyone straight. Before that, people would come and then sit patiently in our great room for their turn to be with Thom.

By then, he could really only spend a significant amount of time with two people in the morning, then nap, and then one or two in the afternoon, and then nap again before family time in the evening. However, sometimes several people would come together for a brief visit, or to ask a question, or just to say goodbye.

One time, a whole crew of Caitlin's History Day friends came in the bedroom to say "Hi" to her Dad after a History Day event.

Holy cow! I forgot to tell you what happened when Thom couldn't be Caitlin's support person for the National History Day in Maryland.

Our friend, Sharon's, two daughters, Kathryn and Carolyn, were also final contenders. She offered to take Caitlin with them to their final performances.

Caitlin called us after each round of the competition as she won Monday through Wednesday. Eventually, she was in line for the last round and although the sisters had gotten "bopped out," they were her support team going into the finals. Everyone was excited about Caitlin's chances, except Caitlin.

"I feel so lucky to have made it this far," she said with true contentment. With that Carolyn said, "Well, someone has to be in first place, why not you?"

Everyone had seen Caitlin's performance so many times that we all had it memorized. It really was fabulous. The problem was that it was Wednesday night. The graduation from eighth grade was Thursday night in Connecticut and the award ceremony for National History Day was Friday in Maryland.

Sharon drove all the girls home Thursday morning and somehow her daughters talked her into driving back down to Maryland at 2 a.m. that night! They all wanted to see who won and where Caitlin placed. The sisters' performance was in the video category and they were proficient with the video camera, so later on Thom and I got to see the whole thing thanks to their skills.

They arrived at the ceremony just as it was opening. We saw the girls and Sharon all sitting, talking in the bleachers, and the parade of all the states' contestants, followed by the announcement of the winners for second and third place. After each one Caitlin would say, "Awe, I didn't make it." Then as she heard her name announced as first place winner, we were deafened by the screams of joy, not only from her and around her, but also in the whole auditorium. Caitlin flew down the bleachers and up onto the stage to receive her trophy.

Her face was radiant as she held that medal up over her head for all to see. It felt just like the Olympics. That high was just what she needed. We all needed that. In fact, the only time I ever saw Thom cry was when he saw Caitlin totally "nail" her performance.

The history crew had some gathering the night they stopped in. At first, it was a little awkward for a bunch of teenagers to be standing around a man who was dying in bed, but Thom was so interested in their projects. After his questions everyone was talking, laughing and cracking jokes just like this was an everyday occurrence. The proud look on Caitlin's face was a sight to behold. The fact that her friends wanted to see her Dad, and that he made them feel comfortable, was beyond mood elevating.

———————————— ✦ ————————————

As 2003 began, Thom no longer had the energy to go to the Monday and Wednesday AA meetings. However, as long as he could physically push himself, he continued to go to his Friday night meeting. It was his favorite one.

In order to get to the meeting, he would rest for the hour before. Then I would warm up the car and back it up to the front door so the passenger door was right next to the front door. I would wheel him to the front door and help him walk the few steps to the car, throw the wheelchair in the back, and drive to the church. Then reverse the routine to get him into the meeting hall.

It was a real privilege for me to attend the last three or four meetings he went to. The members would clear some chairs away from the main table to make room for Thom's wheelchair.

During introductions all the regulars would say their first name and add "I'm an alcoholic." When it came to me, Thom told me to state my first name and add that I was a visitor, but everyone knew who I was.

Passages were read aloud from *The Big Book* and everyone took a turn, even me. I was so nervous that when my turn came I got flustered and flubbed a few sentences. After the reading, certain people volunteered their interpretation of the reading and how it related to them personally or how it could relate to alcoholism in general.

When Thom gave his thoughts on the reading, you could have heard a pin drop. There was such reverence in the room for the bald, shrunken alcoholic in the wheelchair. He could only speak softly and slowly, but everyone hung on to his every word. Despite his physical fading, his spirituality shone through his bright, piercing, dark brown eyes. He would look out at individual people as he spoke.

Thom said, "What I think this means to us alcoholics is," and he went on to interpret the passage. Their eyes were glued on him and several people were shaking their heads in agreement.

It was as if, through his words, he could physically touch each person. They wanted something from him. They wanted the clarity of vision the dying man had, the one who was an alcoholic, just like them. They knew he would steer them right and tell them like it really was. They were counting on him now more than ever before. He seemed surprised that they were looking up to him, that he had some power now that he was dying that he didn't have before. He didn't see that.

Thom wouldn't take any pain pills before he went to AA, so we had agreed that when he was tired or in too much pain, he would look at me and roll his eyes toward the door. Immediately, I would wheel him out to the car knowing he had pushed it to the limit. Someone always got up to help me get Thom in the car. Each meeting, we left earlier and earlier. Then he just couldn't sit up any more.

After that, different AA friends came to the house. Some came to visit; others came to stay with him. Some were able to help him to the bathroom or to make him coffee; others just sat quietly waiting while he slept.

You know… It sounds easy, but it's not. You have to be pretty okay with yourself to sit in someone's bedroom when you know they are on their deathbed. Some people were uncomfortable coming in and visiting because it was in our bedroom. (I think before this experience I would have been too.)

If I needed to go out to the office or shop or pick up the girls, I had an AA "sitter list" to choose from. I don't recall ever needing to call anyone though because I always had more offers than I could use.

Often, I would get a call and the speaker would say, "Hi, I'm a friend of Thom's." If the name wasn't familiar, I knew they were from the program. Many times, these were people I had never met or had seen at a meeting maybe once. They came to our house, took off their shoes at the door, then walked into our bedroom in their stocking feet to be with Thom.

I did make one call to the list while Thom's brother, Steve, was here. There was a huge snowstorm and Steve got Thom's four-wheel drive hopelessly stuck in the driveway. All it took was one call, and in 15 minutes three guys arrived to get the car out. I never knew they had a code in AA to help each other. It is part of their selfless giving.

In fact, all of the 12 steps are excellent rules to live by. If followed, they are the key to personal spirituality. The rest of us would do well to have a program like that.

Now, I take an immediate liking to any patient who comes to my office and tells me first off that they are an alcoholic. I know it means they are in the program, that they are sober, and they are working day-by-day to better themselves.

One day, as Thom was meditating in bed, I was sitting up looking through his calendar, I thought how incredible and full these days had become. Thom wanted it this way, but he obviously didn't plan to have this much company in his final days. No one I have ever known had such meaningful and satisfying personal interactions.

Contemplating the wonder of it all I commented to Thom, "Honey?"

"Yeah?"

"Someone should write a book about this. This whole experience of your dying is not like anything I have ever heard about or imagined. I think people would find it quite enlightening."

Thom looked at me, peering over his glasses with that knowing look.

"Don't look at me," I panicked. "I can't type. I can't spell. And I had boyfriends who wrote my college papers for me."

He wouldn't stop looking at me in that way that says, *So what?*

"You already have a title for it."

"I do?"

"Yeah. It's called 'Living with a Dead Man.'"

At the time, I had no idea if I could write a book, but for months afterward incredible vignettes would come to mind and I'd think, *That should be in the book* (even if I didn't write it).

That's how this book was born. Did he really know I would do it?

It Takes a Village

"My greatest fear in life is NOT dying." – *Ronald East*, whose mother "lived" in a nursing home for 10 years after a debilitating stroke

Outside of the bedroom, a whole world was being impacted by what was going on inside the bedroom. This orchestration of activities took a lot of volunteers. I am still unsure of how this all happened, but I do remember the people who showed up to help.

Allen was driving everyone by then. He picked up and dropped off most visitors at the airport in Hartford, except Steve who he drove to and from the train station.

Allen had lived in Southbury all his life. He went to school with my oldest brother, Joe. Back then it was a really small town. It hadn't been that long since the school had moved out of a one-room schoolhouse. We all went to the same grammar school and played in the same baseball and football games (otherwise, there weren't enough players to make a team). We knew one another and observed each other growing up from a close distance.

Allen had quit drinking and smoking after his throat cancer. He was one of the lucky ones. He only wound up with a raspy voice, chronic cough and emphysema. It never stopped him from talking though. He was a modern-day version of the town crier.

Whenever we would fly anywhere, we loved to have Allen drive us to and from the airport. It was a chance to reminisce as well as to get the real local news. At that time, I got all the news I needed from Allen and NPR radio. In the end, I wasn't so sure I even needed NPR.

———————————— ❦ ————————————

Wendy, my office manager and friend, did a lot of organizing from the office. People would call her and ask what they could do to help me.

At first, so much food arrived she had to give some of it to the soup kitchen in the nearby city. Then she made a rotation of people to bring food and placed it on the calendar. Only one meal per day either by nurses, teachers, friends or family. Meals that could be eaten now, meals that could be frozen, and meal gift cards from Villarina's.

One time, Wendy suggested to my friend, John, that a good time for his treat of a catered salmon dinner was when Thom's Dad was here. Great timing and outrageously delicious.

In case you have forgotten, Thom was the cook. I hadn't cooked in 16 years! One afternoon as I was doing the laundry, changing the beds, checking on Thom and helping the girls with homework, I thought, *I wonder what's for dinner?* Then it dawned on me, *Oh my God, I am doing the cooking.*

Thank God for all those meals. So much happened so quickly I don't think I even thanked everyone. If any of you are reading this now, thank you from the bottom of my heart. You sustained everyone at my house at a time when it was most needed.

One Friday, a crock pot showed up at my office with the meal already cooked. All I had to do was take it home and warm it up in the same pot! Yippee. I knew I could handle that.

On Monday, I sent the cleaned crock pot back with a thank you note inside.

The next Friday, another crock pot meal magically appeared and was again sent back clean with a thank you note where I added, "I think I am okay now," meaning they didn't have to send another meal.

But by each Thursday I was praying for the crock pot to show up again and so it did for at least a dozen Fridays. Honestly, I don't know what I would have done without it.

It wasn't all food either.

One of my patients brought me a huge jar of his honey and another one showed up with a cord of wood for the fireplace. He even brought his grandson to help him stack it.

I guess this sort of community cohesiveness is written about and sometimes is in movies like the "Hallmark Hall of Fame" series, but here it was, happening to my family! I knew I needed help and really had no idea where it was going to come from. I was, and still am, in awe of the ability people have to give. I remain forever grateful.

My big brother, Joe, in his big, puffy Navy down coat with his skullcap pulled down over his ears, often waited patiently for Caitlin to come out to get driven to school. His old Volvo wagon vibrated, while the cold exhaust clouds hung on the end of his tailpipe.

Some mornings, it was my sister-in-law, Deb, who drove Thom to chemo or Caitlin to school. Caitlin loved the rides in Deb's Cadillac.

On other days, it was our neighbor, Don, who drove. I can only vaguely remember talking to all of these wonderful people, so I guess I organized her rides.

Our family friends, Duncan and Francine, "adopted" Justine. Each week, one or the other of them would take her away from the house for drives or outings. These inevitably included visiting horses, bookstores or ice cream shops—sometimes all three. Yup, there was a lot going on in and out of the bedroom.

Caitlin's teachers were wonderful to her. In high school, she usually had three hours of homework a night, but they basically said, "Just keep coming to class. Just show up. Just do the best you can."

Honestly, I don't remember the end of her school year or her exams. I don't even know how they arrived at her final grades that year. I do remember, however, that the head of her school, several teachers, and at least a half dozen of her friends came to Thom's memorial service. It's funny how you never forget those things.

———————————— 🪰 ————————————

One of the many wonderful things at Justine's school was its bereavement group. The school's counselor, Coach, was the group leader. Any student with a family member dying or in jeopardy of dying was invited into the group, as were those students who had experienced a death in the past year.

Justine turned out to be a permanent member of the group. In first grade, my mother (her grandmother) had cancer and died at the end of the year. So she was invited back in the second grade. At the end of second grade, Thom was diagnosed with his cancer. He died at the end of her third grade year, so she was still in the group through fourth grade.

I can only imagine how Coach dealt with Justine and the other lower school students. I do know that over those years the two of them forged a great friendship. By the time she entered fifth grade, Coach asked Justine back. With all of Justine's years of experience, she helped facilitate the feelings of the newer members.

Justine could not have had a better support system in third grade. Not only were Coach and her teacher fantastic at their jobs, but they really liked Justine and she loved them.

Mrs. Greeter was only in her second year of teaching. At the beginning of the year, Justine wasn't so sure she liked her very much. When asked why, she said, "She laughs too much." On further questioning, Justine said Mrs. Greeter herself didn't laugh too much, but she made the students laugh so much that Justine complained that her cheeks hurt.

The stories Mrs. Greeter told were so funny that all the smiling and laughing was doing Justine in. She thought that teachers were supposed to be more serious. I couldn't have picked a better situation for her. School was the perfect balance for what was going on at home.

One warm spring day in early April, Coach and Mrs. Greeter called and asked if they could come over and bring a lunch for Justine. By then, she was missing a lot of school to be with her Dad. She was ecstatic they were coming. She helped push the table on the porch into the sun and chose a bright table cloth and napkins. They brought pizza and root beer, her favorites.

From the kitchen, I could see the three of them out on the sunny porch talking and laughing. After lunch, they brought out a large manila envelope. It was full of handmade cards for her from her classmates.

After they left, Justine showed me all the beautiful cards. Those who knew her well included pictures of horses or other animals. One third grader had lost one of her parents and she told Justine about that in her card. Another one talked about how she felt losing her grandmother.

Some of the cards were so touching. Reading them all was overwhelming. Justine loved it though. She loved the fact that everyone in her grade said something nice to her. The rest of that day was spent in high spirits and was a great contrast to what she had been feeling. She was whistling and laughing again. The visit and the cards were the most powerful boost for a grieving eight-year-old child.

As Thom started to sleep more, there were times when we would just be resting in bed together at any time of the day. I wanted to be near him all the time now, especially as I could feel him fading away. One afternoon, as Thom was resting or meditating (it was hard to tell which he was doing now), I thought about Justine and how difficult this whole process was for her.

What could I do for my daughter to ease her pain? In my mind's eye, I saw her in the riding ring or in the green fields bareback on one of the horses from our local riding stable. I knew being anywhere in the vicinity of a horse was the one thing that made her consistently happy.

She had been riding for three years and it was all she wanted to do. She looked forward to each day with a horse the way most kids would anticipate a special trip to the amusement park. She relished everything she learned about them.

Of course, she loved to ride and jump, but she also enjoyed all the chores and the physical contact with the horses. She would have slept in the barn just to be near the horses if I would have let her.

"Honey?" I asked, nudging him from his sleep or whatever he was doing.

"Yeah?" He responded without opening his eyes.

"Honey, you're dying and I need some advice about Justine." Now his eyes were open and he looked with that questioning look.

"She is totally into horses. It's way beyond a passing fancy. I see it in the way she is around them. She lives for the horses. Not only that, but she has a special way with them. There is a real communication between her and the horses. They like her almost as much as she likes them. When she is on a horse in the ring, riding or jumping, it is as if she is one with it. There is something fluid about their forms together—girl and horse are indistinguishable, almost one, not two. It reminds me of an old movie like *Black Velvet* where Elizabeth Taylor's horse can do unbelievable things because of the powerful bond between the two of them."

I was rambling and his eyes were closed again. I tried to get to the point.

"Honey, am I supposed to buy her a horse after you die?"

He thought for a moment, then opened his eyes and looked into mine.

"If she is still passionate about horses, buy her a horse. Too many parents discount their kid's passion. They say things like, 'Kids don't know how much work is involved' or 'It's too expensive' or 'It's just a passing phase.' But if she's passionate, get her a horse."

As soon as he said it, I knew immediately it was the right thing to do.

"I am going to miss all the good advice you give me, especially with Justine. You understand her so well."

I was feeling a little needy and whiney.

"How am I going to communicate with her when you are gone? Give me some tips so I can understand her better. Often times, I don't even get what she is trying to say. I have good intuitions—you know I do—but more often than not, she and I are just on different wavelengths."

"With Justine," he began softly, "you have to understand her intention. Both with what she says and what she does."

I waited, but I didn't get it. There has to be more.

"Her intentions?" I asked.

"Yes," he said it matter-of-factly, like we had talked about this before and he was simply reminding me. I was hoping he was going to say something more insightful or clarify what he meant. I kept waiting.

Then he added, "When you are responding to her you have to know what your intention is for her, both in what you say and what you do."

He said this like it was a simple mathematical equation and now that it was all spelled out, I would get it. Meanwhile I was still hoping he was going to add a crystallizing statement, but now he had his eyes closed. Apparently, he was finished with the explanation.

"So it's all about intentions—intentions from her and intentions from me?" I tenuously replied.

"Yes, that's it." He said it like, *Good, you got it.*

I've got to tell you... I was sitting in bed thinking about how I could apply this new insightful thinking, only nothing came to mind—not one bloody thing. I waited... Nothing.

"Great. You know what? That's just great," I said as I slammed my paper down on the bed. Now I was pissed. If he knew this all along, why didn't he tell me this before? Now he was so close to death, we didn't really have any time for him to teach me this, or for me to practice it until I was comfortable with it.

"You are the only one I know who intuitively understands our daughter and now you're dying. And your parting words are that the key to communicating with her is some psycho-babble bullshit about intentions?"

Now I was freaking out.

"I am not stupid—I'm a doctor for Christ's sake—but I don't get it. She is my daughter too, and I just don't get it, okay? I want to get it, but I don't. This kid is going to go ballistic after you are gone and I am her only hope. And I don't know how to help her!"

I crossed my arms over my chest. "So thanks. Thanks a lot!"

Thom looked at me with a mixture of distress and empathy. "Honey, you will get it. You will. You are stressed right now, but you will get it. I know you will, when you get some time to think about it."

I must have looked pretty skeptical peering into his face where I hoped to catch some clue because then he added, "Have faith. You'll get it."

He patted my hand, apparently in an attempt to sooth my frazzled nerves. He looked at me convincingly and I was really hoping he was right like he usually was, but inside there were no connections happening. There was a void.

It didn't feel like there were going to be any connections going on in the near future either. I just wanted to practice this new way of thinking a few times. I wanted the security of knowing there was a pathway in my brain that had been tried correctly at least once. Once, before he was gone.

When would that be?

The doctor in me knew we were nearing the end. I just didn't know how near.

Apparently Thom did.

It was about 2 or 3 a.m. Why we were both awake, I don't remember. I do remember though that our entire bed was bathed in moonlight pouring in through the west window. The full moon shining was like one huge headlight suspended above the horizon.

"Wow, look at that," I said. "Isn't that beautiful?"

Thom put his thin arm around me and whispered, "Let's just lie here and snuggle while we watch our last moon set together."

As I laid my head on his chest, my mind flew to near panic. He knew. He knew his death was less than one month away. I choked back the tears and panic.

He had learned to live in the moment. I wanted it too, desperately. I wanted this moment with him. This moment watching the most incredible full moon setting I had ever seen. This moment with my husband—a moment that would never come again.

I got my moment. It took only a deep breath and letting go of every other thought except to stay firmly attached to Thom and the moon. His warm chest rose and fell under my head. I heard his heart beating in my ear and felt his breath on my temple as he kissed me. I could smell his scent. I rubbed my face in his neck and snuggled closer into his embrace.

We were mesmerized by the moonlight and the moment of togetherness. We stayed there until the moon had completely set. There was no room for anything else. The experience of living fully in the present requires one's complete attention—nothing more, nothing less.

Reconciliation

"By the time you get to a place where you can get the answers, the answers don't matter anymore." – Pete Bette

Sarah's second visit after Christmas was in stark contrast to the first one. That one had been in the summer when we were all hopeful. Although Thom was bald, he looked and acted like his normal self.

This time, Thom was debilitated from both the chemo and the cancer. He had lost weight, he was pale and he was anything but his usual teasing cocky self. She came with her nine-year-old, Mario, and her boyfriend, Scott.

What a breath of fresh air they were. She cooked, spent time with the girls and me as well as Thom. Scott played with the kids and helped where he could. He even cleaned the whole basement.

One day, Thom said he wanted to go to Costco! *What a great idea, an outing.* Scott came with us because Thom could get droopy on occasion and I needed help getting him in and out of the wheelchair.

Off we went in high spirits. Scott wheeled Thom past aisles with bright-colored clothing to the meat counter at the back of the store. Thom wanted some New York strip steaks, his favorite. It was all so much fun until we were coming back from the meat counter and I noticed Thom leaning forward in the chair, his knuckles white from squeezing the arm rests.

"What's the matter?" I asked.

"I think I have to lie down." He answered feebly.

He couldn't tell me if he was in pain or nauseated or what. I think it was everything, including a big dose of how debilitated he was. It was much more obvious out in the real world. It was clear that this was his last trip to his beloved Costco. I bet they even saw a small dent in their revenue after Thom stopped shopping there.

It was during that visit that Sarah decided to come back and stay with Thom until the end. She was very definite about that. It was a huge sacrifice for her, and meant she would have to leave Mario and Scott back in California for an unknown amount of time.

We spoke often on the phone about when she should come back. It was weird trying to tell her exactly when I thought her Dad was going to die, yet I was the one who was the best judge of that. When Thom told me on that moonlit night that it was his last, she made her plans.

Her third and final visit was after everyone had come and gone. He could only sit up in the recliner for short periods of time.

There were a million loving and caring things that she did for her Dad in those last few months, but the thing I will never forget was a conversation she had with her Dad that I witnessed.

It was a night when just the three of us were sitting in the bedroom after dinner. The small wooden table was between us. Thom sat in his recliner. I sat to his right and Sarah was to my right, across from Thom.

We were just kicking back, talking over our empty dinner plates about Sarah's plans to go back to college to finish her degree. She had two more years to complete it. She was doing very well in school. She always had. It was life that was more of a challenge.

Thom was complementing her. "How many single, teenage Moms have gotten into the National Honor Society?" He asked proudly.

"Yeah," I added, "and only three months after going back to high school full-time."

Sarah looked down into her lap as if it held a deep pool of thought. After a minute or two she started to talk. Her voice was husky.

"Dad…" as she looked at her father tears were streaming down her face.

"Yeah, honey?" He looked concerned for this change in her demeanor.

"I want to apologize for being such a difficult child."

"What?" he asked softly.

"When I was a teenager, I know I was really bad. I made things really difficult for you… and I'm really sorry."

Now she was sobbing.

"You didn't deserve it. My being with Mario and having little Mario, living in the barrio—I know it was hard on you. I'm sorry I did it."

Thom was stunned. He couldn't say a word, but clearly she had impacted some deep aching place in his psyche. He looked at Sarah as if she had just told him the most unexpected, but necessary, information he had ever heard. Something he really wanted or needed, but never would have asked for.

Sarah continued, "That's why I worked so hard to get into the National Honor Society. I wanted to prove to you that I was still a good person. I got those grades for you. I knew they meant something to you. I wanted you to be proud of me."

Oh my God, I thought, *she is asking her Dad for forgiveness.*

Looking from Sarah to Thom I could see that they were both tearing up. By that point, I was too paralyzed to move. I was holding my breath. I didn't want to break the spell.

"I was certainly proud of you Sarah and I *never* doubted that you were a good kid." He was not moving, but it was as if he was stroking her face with his words.

"But I wasn't. I was angry. I was stubborn. I was acting out," she sobbed hunched over into her napkin. "I could have been a better daughter. I am so sorry, Dad, especially now."

Thom's expression was a mixture of empathy and sadness.

"Sarah…" It took a few seconds for her to look up at him. "I'm sorry too."

She looked a little confused by that.

"I could have been a better father. I could have done more." The truth was out now, on both sides.

They looked at each other for a time. No words were said, yet something new was happening now. There was a connectedness in their eyes as if blinds were lifted and a direct lifeline between them was established.

Some physical thing was happening to them. It seemed as if some heavy weight or constriction had been removed from the main artery to their hearts and souls. Now nourishment was flooding into an area that was barely subsisting for too long. Their faces were flushed. They stared into each other, speechless.

It was the look of understanding.

It was the look of empathy.

It was the look of unburdening.

It was the look of forgiveness.

The End Is Near

*"As the body shuts down, it is preparing for a gentle death.
Tension has left the room. Now peace is there. Death is miraculous."*
– Mary Jane Glifford, a pediatric nurse who retired,
then worked in a nursing home

In those last few weeks, Thom would float in and out of consciousness. The girls helped give him a bed bath, just like we did before my mother died. We would take one arm or leg out from under the sheets at a time. I would wash, Caitlin would rinse, and I would dry. Then, Justine would massage him with lotion.

I was so grateful that when my mother was dying, we had gotten to bathe her together. At least all these details about dying at home were not so shocking to the girls—and not initially learned on their Dad.

My mother had been a teacher in that way too. In fact, we had some pretty great laughs with her during those bed baths, and she loved the way Justine massaged her, especially her feet.

One day, while my mother was still able to creep from the bed to the couch, she asked what I thought was an odd question.

"Marianne, how will I die?"

Holy crap! She didn't know?

179

When I thought back on it, all four of my grandparents died in the hospital. I don't even know if anyone was there with them. I guess that was where everyone went to die back then.

"Well Mom, you will start drifting, somewhat like when you are asleep. You will spend some time here with us and some time over there. Then you will spend more time there and less here. Pretty soon you will be over there more and more."

She listened intently.

"Then, one time you will just decide to just stay there and not come back. You will be content there. You will feel like you are at home."

"Oh," that was all she said.

I promised her she would not feel any pain, which consoled her. Although her body did not co-operate with a totally peaceful plan, I believe her spirit did.

Now Thom was drifting. As Thom slipped in and out of a coma, the three girls and I were by his side constantly. Rarely, he would ask for a sip of water, but most of the time he was not conscious.

He was on an IV of pain medication monitored by the VNA hospice. Hopefully, he would go the gentlest way possible. Already the unconscious times were increasing. Soon there were no more conscious times at all.

Our lives centered around the bedroom. We played cribbage in the bedroom, watched movies, and slept there too.

One day, Sarah and Caitlin were on my side of the bed playing cards and laughing when Sarah made this noise like Gollum, that character from *The Hobbit*. It was a real guttural noise and for the first time that day Thom opened his eyes and stared at the girls with a look that said, "What the hell was that?"

From then on, we were all more conscious of what we said in the bedroom. They say that dying people can hear you, but sometimes you forget that fact, especially when hours and days go by and the person starts looking a bit like part of the furniture.

When it was clear that Thom had no conscious times left, the three girls and I set up a vigil. We knew the end was near. One of us was in the room at all times. Those last ten days of Thom's life, when he was in a coma, were the most grueling. Each day, the house became increasingly quiet.

We all knew he was close to death now. No talking. No communicating. He was slowly and constantly drifting away. It felt as if he was tethered on a string like a helium balloon and he was being let out more and more, hour by hour. Individually, Sarah, Caitlin and Justine and I would go in and out of the bedroom to check on Thom's status.

Somewhere in the middle of those days, the hospice nurse visited. We wanted to do what was right for Thom, but we were all weary of the bedroom vigil. Were we right to stay by his side constantly? Was there anything else we should consider?

The hospice nurse Thom chose for himself was the same one who helped us with my mother's death. He really liked her. She was so helpful and easy to talk to. She could answer any question we had. But she couldn't answer the one we wanted to know most.

"When will he die?"

"Each person picks their own time," she answered. "Sometimes the person will wait until everyone is there. Sometimes they pick that one moment when they are alone."

After speaking with her, we decided to stop living in the bedroom. Collectively, we ended the vigil. It was an act of self-preservation. We each wanted to hold on to those last few shreds of our sanity.

I knew Thom would wait for all of us to be there. I just knew it. Ten or twenty times a night I would wake from my sleep and reach over to feel his pulse. *Beat, beat, beat, beat.*

I'd go back to sleep. In the beginning, he would squeeze my hand in response. Later on, nothing. A warm hand, a steady pulse that was all.

We were constantly in and out of the room. Out when we couldn't stand it in there anymore and in when we couldn't stand staying out.

We played endless games of solitaire and cribbage in the kitchen. We actually got to the point of barely even talking. Cryptic comments like "No change" were shortened even further to a simple shake of the head.

Caitlin and Sarah made frequent runs to Starbucks in an effort to break the tension, get away, and just get silly. Justine watched one Disney video after the other. I cleaned.

All these activities got old quickly. The waiting was oppressive.

No one called. Everyone knew how close to death he was. They certainly didn't want to be put in the strange position of asking, "Is he dead yet?" Really, I guess it was better that way.

After all the visitors, the house was so damn quiet. On Day Seven, I called Regina and vented my frustration, telling her I couldn't stand it anymore.

"It seems like forever now, but when it's over, it will seem like the blink of an eye," she said. It seemed impossible to believe at that moment, but I knew she was right. Once Thom was actually dead, everything would change in the snap of a finger.

The bedroom always seemed to be a part of every trip I made in the house. If I was cooking, before I sat down to eat I would check on Thom. If I was playing cribbage and went to the bathroom, I checked on Thom.

Sometimes I would find myself by his side and not even remember what I was doing. This time I don't know what brought me in or how long I stood there looking at his rising and falling chest. Looking at him, I saw the sunken cheeks and slender body, now at least 80 pounds lighter.

What a pathetic body. Even if we found a miracle cure, there's no way you could make it in that body. You have to die, honey. You have to go.

No matter how hard it is to see a body like that, it is that vision that lets you know this person has to die now.

182

One day, while Sarah was on the phone with Mario, I couldn't find Caitlin and Justine. The only place I hadn't looked was the office above the garage. As I approached the steps, I could hear a lot of commotion. When I opened the door, there they were jumping from couch to chair and onto big pillows that were strewn around the floor.

"Hey you guys, what are you doing?" I asked, surprised.

"We are having *fun*, Mom," Justine answered from a midair front handspring.

"I can see that," I said, watching their gymnastics in amazement. They stopped almost breathless while Justine spelled it out for me.

"We can't stand it anymore! Dad's dying and he takes all your attention. It's making us crazy. So we are just getting our anger out and having fun."

It was one of those moments when you wish you could split yourself into two so you could do both tasks that needed to be done at the same time, and do it well—time with my dying husband or time with my grieving kids?

"You are right. I do spend a lot of time with Dad. But Dad is not only your father. He is my husband, my best friend, and my partner. I will do any and everything I can for him so he can have the best death possible. I don't expect you to understand this, but that's okay."

At that, a flushed-faced Caitlin demonstrated the couch-to-chair jumping routine. Justine did a handstand and then fell over backward onto appropriately placed pillows as her rumpled hair followed.

"Well, I'm glad you figured out a way to take care of yourselves. Just don't get hurt, okay?" I said, but also I realized that my girls were more resilient than I gave them credit for.

It was a lucky thing too that I had girls who were so in touch with their feelings, since my mothering skills at that point were totally out to lunch. "It looks great, sweethearts. Carry on."

"Come on, Mom. Join us," they invited me. Under any other circumstances, I would have.

"I'd like to, but I can't. I just plain don't feel like I can."

I felt so alienated, so removed, so absolutely *other*.

There was no other choice but to go through this part of the process—not knowing how or when the end would come, fearing it and now finally craving it. Knowing there were few precious hours left and wanting it to be over, to be free of it all. Wanting to be on the getting-our-lives-together-without-Thom side of things. Hoping it would feel better, but knowing at least it would feel different. We wouldn't be sitting around drinking tea and playing cribbage all night, or sitting, standing or lying in a room with an almost dead man.

At least that would be over. His body would be gone. We would make our plans without him, however painful that would be. But they would be our plans—our future. We would be moving on, away from this stuck spot.

Sarah could go back to Mario and Scott, and have her life back in California. The girls could go back to school and eventually I could plan to go back to work. I would, like them, be lulled back into a sense of normalcy by doing what I have done my whole adult life, doing what I loved and what I was good at. It would feed my hungry soul. Even being "less than normal" would be a good move from where I was now, stuck waiting for death.

We could have made it easier on ourselves, I guess. I could have put him in a nursing home and gotten some relief from the intensive 24/7 care. But I couldn't let myself do that. I made a promise and I was going to keep it. When he was gone, I would not really be sleeping alone. I would be sleeping with my conscience, and that made all the difference.

On the eighth day after Thom slipped into a coma, I became—well, I became unhinged. The medical term for it is *decompensated*. I was there. It was a total meltdown. I doubt anyone could relate to it unless they had been in a similar bizarre place. I always thought it was thoughtful and truly the "right thing to do" to have someone die at home, in their own bed, comforted by their own things and surrounded by the people they loved. It sounded almost storybook perfect. For the record, there is one extremely significant missing piece in this equation. It is the primary caretaker, in this case, me.

I hadn't left the house for weeks. I had forgotten to take myself into account (a bad habit of mine). I thought I could go through anything for Thom. After all, he was dying. I wasn't. But there is only so long you can survive in the desert without water, no matter who you are.

Pacing around the house, I started having conversations with myself out loud. I was in and out of the bedroom constantly. I started to think he was going to last a month like this and then *I* would be the one in the hospital, in the psych ward. Visions of me in a straightjacket, drugged and drooling almost started to seem like a relief. I began to feel held captive by a living dead man. I was ready for him to go. *Why was he still here? Why hadn't he left yet?* Knowing Thom, I should have known that he would take an excessive amount of time to die.

I found myself retreating to the closet again for another private phone call, this time to Kert.

"Kert, I am losing it. I am going stark raving mad. Honestly I don't think I can take it anymore," I whined. "How long can a young man with a healthy heart go on living in a coma? Isn't there something you can do to help him along?"

He admonished me to be careful who was around to hear me speaking like this, especially the kids.

"All we can do is keep him comfortable."

We spoke about his medications and vital signs. He said all he could do was change his pain medicines, which he did. Did I really think he was going to become Dr. Kevorkian? Did I really want him to?

Changing his medications made no difference. Zip.

If you were coming undone, where would you go to become calm, cool and collected? For me it was the garden.

Walking around the garden I tried to focus on the "now." I looked at the blue sky and I could feel the sun's warmth on my sweater. The

185

birds were singing and there were loads of green shoots breaking the surface of the ground after their long winter's sleep. The daffodils were so incredibly yellow, the hyacinths so fragrant, and many other small groupings of bulbs trying to bloom and open. The trees in the fern garden wore their red and chartreuse tones, getting ready to bud. Even the grass was trying to get into the act.

I wondered if on some level Thom chose to die during the spring? It was impossible to ignore the hopeful life and beauty of spring's orchestration, and almost impossible to stay disconnected or down.

I don't know how long I was out there, but staying in the now saved me. Soon I was back in the bedroom with a more peaceful point of view. I'd had a mini-vacation.

I stood at the foot of my bed looking at the corpse-man-husband barely attached to life. Questions floated through my mind.

Is this the man I have known?

What is he waiting for?

Is he in some timeless place, where "here" doesn't matter?

If we don't matter, why doesn't he release us?

Is he staying for Justine?

Will these few hours or days really make a difference?

I want you to go.

I did not speak out loud, but began to address him.

I'm ready.

Go.

Just go.

Let go and go to heaven or wherever.

We will make it without you. We already are!

This is bad form, hanging on like this.

Then it hit me.

Who the hell am I to tell you when to die? Here I am stuck in my time with my own thinking. I'm frustrated with all the unanswered *questions and the unknowns in my future. I am scared to go on without you. It was **you** I could talk to, **you** who witnessed and interpreted my life for me (sometimes in painful accuracy). Now you will be gone.*

But you know what? I am going to be okay. You may be outta here, but I am not. I am still here. I think it will be some time before I will be leaving these girls. We are going our separate ways now, you and me. The team is breaking up. I am thankful for what I had. You enriched my life beyond measure.

If I think about it, I am pretty darn lucky, even though you are dying right now. I'm grateful for what I learned from you. I've gotten enough to get by pretty well on my own now. If not, I guess I'll fake it.

Okay. Deep breath.

I'm alright now.

I'll give it over to you.

Take your time.

Take whatever it is that you need.

I surrender.

I surrender to you.

I surrender to the process.

It is what it is.

*I **will** be okay.*

I felt the tension wash off me like the garden hose washes the summer dirt off my legs. I looked around our bedroom as if I were seeing it for the first time. What insights could a person gain by looking into this dying man's room just now?

On the Oriental rug by the sliding door overlooking the forest porch was an inflatable air mattress where two sets of blankets and pillows lay rumpled. Some type of a sleepover, you would guess.

In the corner was a small recliner next to a table and lamp, with wooden chairs placed on either side of it. It's as if someone had been sitting there telling stories and others had come to listen.

On top of the oak chest nearby was a series of pictures. There was a beautiful college-aged woman with long sandy hair and, next to her, a smaller picture of a young boy in a soccer shirt who looked a lot like her. In a large frame, were two girls in red velvet dresses. One was about five years old, and had long dark hair with piercing eyes. The other was a laughing colleen of about ten.

On the antique mahogany dresser was an old tilt-top lead mirror. Stuck under the edge of the frame were handmade cards from children. "Get well, Dad," inside a red heart with a teardrop on the bottom. "I love you and I'll miss you, Dad," on a rainbow arching between two clouds.

On the surface of the dresser was a leather box holding a watch with a leather wristband, car keys on an old Tiffany key chain, credit cards and a worn black leather wallet.

An unusual handmade Native American rug hung over the bed. It was a powerful spiritual piece. It had a teepee and a brass drum with birds flying straight up to the heavens.

In the bed was a corpse-like body. He would never again wonder what time it was or where he had left his car keys. He wouldn't see the smiling faces when the braces come off. Many sports games and concerts would go by in his absence. He wouldn't be going for college visits, nor high school graduations. He would never walk any of those three girls down the aisle on their wedding day. That much was clear with just a glimpse around the room.

Could he be a Native American? Whoever he was, it appeared he had a full life. A lot of living had gone on right here in this room, too. Now it seemed suspended, timeless.

Funny how I came in mad, telling him to go. Now I realized that time was much less relevant than I had thought. Grateful, I surrendered to the process that had little to do with me. Perhaps this was what he was waiting for: my death acceptance.

On Day Number Ten, we all left the house to see a movie. Now we were all openly talking about him dying.

"Why doesn't he just let go? Why doesn't he just die?"

We all asked these questions of each other. It was around 10 p.m. when we finished the movie and slowly drifted into the bedroom. He looked just the same.

Once again, I felt his pulse. This time it was irregular.

Justine said, "I think his breathing is different."

"Hey you guys, something is happening. His pulse is all weird," I said.

Everyone froze as we looked at each other and then at Thom. It was what we never wanted before, and what we all wanted now but were scared to have happen.

As we all looked on like statues, his breathing became shallow and shallower. Then it just stopped. So too his pulse faded and then was simply gone. It was as if someone had just let go of a long tether and its balloon drifted away.

We looked at each other. *Now what?* We had focused on this point for so long and now we were here. We didn't really plan what we would do at this exact time after his death. It was as if we were lost at the end of a path.

We each took our time to kiss his silent face goodbye. We all stood back from the bed as reality sunk in deeper. It was a dramatic change in a subtle way. Even a weak candle sends light into a darkened room, but when that light is snuffed out, it's totally dark.

As if on cue, we started to back away from the bed. Each of us breathing a sigh of relief. We were all looking at Thom's body, so obviously empty now. It was like Thom had gone and this shell was all that was left behind.

"Thank God," I said. "It's over."

The girls just nodded.

"Let's go. I'm putting the kettle on."

As we left the bedroom, I couldn't keep from adding, "I am not sleeping in here tonight."

Like shell-shocked stragglers leaving the battlefield, we shuffled into the kitchen and sat around the table. Our entire reality changed in the flip of a switch. We knew it would, but now the *knowing* was all different.

We each sat quietly sipping our drinks as our new reality settled on us.

It was Justine who said, "Let's hold hands and say grace over our hot chocolate."

We took her sage advice and held each other's hands and bowed our heads as she continued.

"We know our Dad is in heaven now and he will watch over us. We already miss him, but we are glad his pain is done. Amen."

"Amen."

"Amen."

"Amen."

The Morning After

"When you are at the bedside of a dying person, you suddenly realize there is no place in the world you would rather be." – Anne Dooney

When my mother was dying, a patient of mine who was a hospice nurse told me about the "home wake." One of the big advantages to dying at home, as she saw it, was that you could have an old-fashioned wake. The dead person is kept at home for awhile so that the loved ones can have time to grieve right there at the bedside in the privacy and comfort of their own home. That way each person could take their own time. She felt that this was especially important if there was not going to be a traditional wake and church burial.

It worked out really well when my mother was cremated. Those who did not want to go in didn't, and those who wanted to take their time, did. It was surprising that the goodbyes, which took place in her bedroom with her lying there perfectly still in her own bed, were more comforting than I ever would have thought.

Thom also wanted to be cremated, so we planned on doing the same home wake with him. We would wait to send his body off until everyone was ready.

Sarah and Caitlin were finished first. Then they were off to Starbuck's in about two minutes. Later in the morning, after several more visits to the bedroom, I was ready. It was amazingly weird, but great all the same, to be able to go back in and look at Thom's body and not feel his spirit in it anymore.

I'm sure there are many spiritual discussions and explanations for this feeling. Marilyn, my 80-year-old yoga teacher, told me that yogis that were well-practiced could just "drop the body" when they wanted to die. What a great visual image. As if the spirit had somewhere else to go and the body had to be left behind.

With just that difference in terminology, a very different vision of what was happening took hold of my psyche. Thom, as I knew him, was not here anymore. I tried to "feel" his spirit, to see if he was still hanging around like you always hear. But honestly, I could feel nothing.

Here now in my bedroom was an empty body. I caught myself making a distinction between what my husband was and his body, which was a worn-out shell.

The difference between a life force being present and it being absent is more dramatic when your loved one's body is in their own home. It could not have been more obvious, more definite or more final—like looking into an empty carafe that once held a fabulous wine, the vessel cannot hold more than the essence. Thom was now a memory of what was once a part of this life.

Justine, however, was definitely *not* ready. As it turned out, she was no way even *near* ready. In and out she went, almost relieved each time that he was still there, despite his being dead. She later asked for undisturbed time by herself with her Dad. She was in the bedroom for quite some time. I heard her talking, crying and at one point she was singing. It was almost impossible to give her space.

It had been very important for her to have a single rose at Thom's bedside while he was dying. Now, she plucked the petals one-by-one and made a crown of them around his head, leaving one off near his left ear, "So his spirit can get out," she said.

Where did she get that idea?

Then she placed the rest of the petals in a line down the center of his chest. Finally, she came out and insisted I take some pictures of her with Thom's body and the rose petals. It was disturbing to me to be taking those pictures, but I focused on what was important to Justine. I was sure Thom could not have cared less.

Neither Justine nor I have ever looked at the pictures I took that day.

The hospice nurse came around 10:30 a.m. and she officially pronounced Thom as dead, even though it had really occurred twelve hours earlier. She gave me the number of the crematorium and told me to call when I wanted them to pick up his body.

Shortly after that, I asked Justine if she was ready for them to come.

"No," she answered emphatically.

After an hour, I asked the same question again.

"No!" She was now obstinate. "If anybody touches my Dad, I'll cut their hands off."

Each time I asked, I thought perhaps she needed a little more time to adjust to the whole death thing. But on the third time I thought I would take a different approach.

"Honey, pretty soon Dad's body is going to start to stink. We can't have that, so I'm going to call the guys to come and take his body away."

Through clenched teeth she warned, "If anybody touches my Dad I'm going to kick them in the pee-pee."

Oh great! My husband is dead and my eight-year-old is going to start a brawl with the mortuary attendants, just great.

At a loss, I went back to the garden to figure out what to do. It was important that this go smoothly for Justine. Once again a new tact. I reminded her that this is what her Dad's wishes were for himself and that we had to respect them.

Justine wanted to know why we couldn't take Thom's body to the mortuary ourselves. This conjured up the weirdest images of us driving around with his stiff body laid out in the back of my station wagon, and me trying to explain the situation to a police officer if we got stopped.

"My husband just died and we are dropping his body off at the crematorium."

Next, she wanted to know why we couldn't just bury him in the backyard in the pet grave yard next to our dead bunny and the parakeet. Now I was flashing on getting my hands on a backhoe and digging his grave where Fluffy and Tweety are buried. No, this was not allowed, but there were options.

We could put his ashes somewhere special after we got them back from the crematorium. How would she feel about that? It seemed to make her feel better that his final resting place could be here at home. I guessed that was what she wanted. I mean, really—who knows what goes on in the mind of a grieving child?

Then I got the great idea of *how* to put my question to her.

"Justine, by the way, when do *you* think it would be a good time for those guys to come and pick up Dad's body?"

"Oh, about 3:30," she says as if she is mentally checking her schedule.

Thank God!

"Okay, honey, that's a little over an hour from now."

Maybe she needed a little control over something in this whole out-of-control situation.

"Are you okay with that?" I checked.

"It's okay, Mom," and off she skips.

I was emphatic with the mortuary attendants that they *not* come before 3:30. They did not. But needless to say, I was still a little nervous when they arrived. They were two young college-aged guys in blue suits and ties. They probably just saw this as a well-paying job to get them through college, nothing more.

Sarah and Caitlin were out having coffee, as usual. Justine was by my side as the guys got out of the van and stepped into the atrium. I couldn't help looking at their crotches and thinking they had no idea what mortal danger they were in if had they arrived early.

At that point, Justine pulled on my sleeve and conspiratorially gestured for me to step into the bedroom. Suddenly, I felt protective of the poor college guys just trying to do their job.

"Justine, you are not thinking about kicking those guys in the pee-pee, are you?"

"Mom!" she says in that *get real* kind of way.

"Oh good. Just checking" I added. "Now, what?"

"Mom, Dad can't go to the cremation place in those old pajamas."

"It's okay, honey. It really doesn't matter. It's all going to be ashes soon anyway."

"Mom!" she said emphatically, "I want Dad to leave in clean PJs."

"Okay. Do you want to help me change him, then?" I figured that would stop her.

"Yes."

Oh God, here we go.

So I asked the guys to step outside and give us a few minutes. It was a really strange thing to change Thom into those clean PJs. Justine wanted him to have on his old favorites.

We had done so much care-taking of Thom's body that it didn't seem to bother her, but it sure bothered me. Putting those clothes and socks on his cold stiff body with my eight-year-old is one of those memories I wish I didn't have. None of it freaked out Justine, however. She was a kid on a mission. We paused looking at him in his favorite old pajamas.

"Are you ready now, honey?" I paused.

She was standing there surveying Thom.

"He really does need to go."

"Yes, Mom, I'm ready," she stated in a definitive tone.

"Okay," I said to them, "He's ready."

I was so thankful that thus far this had gone along uneventfully. They had a collapsible aluminum gurney that they popped open and rolled into the bedroom.

Justine followed them in and they looked repeatedly over their shoulders at her as she followed them. I doubt they'd had to deal much before with an eight-year-old watching them.

She stood her ground as they rolled the gurney over to Thom's side of the bed. They lifted his stiff, light body effortlessly and placed it on the gurney in the middle of the black body bag. The guy at the feet zipped it up from the feet all the way up to the waist where the guy at the head then zipped it down over Thom's face. Then the young man at the head shot a glance over at Justine and immediately unzipped the black bag back down to reveal her Dad's face, as if he knew Justine needed that done.

As they wheeled Thom out of the room, she followed behind them and then right out to the van. I started to tremble with the anticipation that something dramatic was about to take place. As they put the gurney legs up, the whole thing folded easily into the back of the van. I was poised to grab Justine in what I feared would be the brawl she had threatened earlier, but she acquiesced. We stood together gazing into the back of the van.

"Bye-bye, Daddy," she said as she waved into the back of the van. The two young men were standing by each door, waiting solemnly for Justine to finish her goodbyes.

"Bye, honey," I said, following suit.

The guys looked questioningly at me. I looked at Justine and nodded to them. Then they closed the doors. She watched as they drove up the driveway until they were out of sight.

After that, Justine and I staggered into the house, landed on the couch, and melted into each other's arms. The rest of that day was a blank.

———————— ✦ ————————

Since we had the ceremony planned months before Thom died, everything would be the way he wanted it. It was much easier to follow through with his plans than to try to come up with an idea of what we thought he would have liked. It gave us all a unified focus and left us feeling like we were still able to do something special for Thom. Maybe it also gave us the feeling of him still being close to us in those days leading up to and including the service. This was how he planned it.

Sarah decided not to speak, which made sense since she knew very few of the people who would attend. Caitlin and Justine both wanted to say something about their Dad to the congregation of their family and friends.

In the first day or two after Thom died, they were busy writing their speeches and working with Bonnie. I had no idea what they were going to say, but since they were with Bonnie I had no worries. They even went down to the church to practice delivering their speeches from behind the pulpit.

Bonnie was first my patient, then my friend and, for that week, my minister. I was so grateful to her for showing up and giving the girls tasks to do. Caitlin and Justine were very happy to be directed by Bonnie. When they were with her, I completely let go of thinking about them. Handy, to have an ordained minister as a friend!

Bonnie had come up with the idea of the girls making a handout for the service. She suggested they print them in different colors and have them on a table at the church's entrance. The girls loved that idea. They were on a mission. It's surprising how comforting having a purpose can be.

"How about we put some pictures on it?" Bonnie asked.

"Yeah," they answered in unison.

"Don't you girls have some pictures you have drawn yourselves?" she asked.

Justine presented a happy stick figure she had made for her Dad a few years before. Caitlin offered a colored pencil drawing she too had made for Thom that he had framed. It was a picture of a house tied up in a bow. Printed in her little girl handwriting next to the picture was his favorite saying, "Daddy says we should live in the present."

LIVING WITH A DEAD MAN

These two images were used to decorate the outside of the memorial bulletin.

The inside of the bulletin contained the order of the hymns, talks, Caitlin's piano piece, drumming and remembrances, and on the back were the words to the Native American hymn for group singing: Wakantanka Taku Nitawa (Many and Great, O God, Are Your Works). Thom had remembered this from his childhood.

Sarah and I were busy calling everyone, while Caitlin and Justine worked on their project. Giving people the news of Thom's passing was exhausting.

The hardest one was Thom's father. He had so little to say and I didn't know what to add to make it any easier on him. It was one of those times when you truly are at a loss for words. All I could say was, "I love you, Dad. I will keep in touch." Next I called Thom's brother, Steve. It was the weirdest conversation.

"Steve, it's Marianne."

"I know. He's gone," he answered.

"You do?" I was really surprised.

"Yep, he was here."

"He was... There?"

"Yeah. I was sitting on a park bench last night looking at the ocean and he came and sat there right next to me."

"You're kidding," I said, amazed.

I knew he wasn't kidding. The rhetorical question was all I could say as I digested the meaning of his words.

"Did he say anything to you?"

"No. It was like one of those spirit things where you got the idea of what he wanted to say."

"Okay... What was it?"

"He wanted me to know he was fine, maybe even more than fine. He was happy."

"Wow. What time was it?"

198

When we figured out the time difference, it was the same time he had died. Trippy, we thought. Very trippy. But also just like Thom.

I called my cousin, Bob, and he called his sister, Mary Ann. Growing up in either of our families wasn't easy and sometimes she, Bob and I had to band together to survive. It seemed like that again now. Mary Ann and I are six months apart in age, but she went to medical school right out of college while I waited four years. She has been a long-distance support for me most of my life. Sometimes I think I am a doctor because of her advice. She had a habit of shedding a positive light on my life.

When Thom, the girls and I went on our annual camping trip to the Northern California Redwoods, we would stop at Mary Ann and Dick's in Marin, near San Francisco. Sometimes, it was at the last minute, but we were always welcomed. I still cherish those visits we all had together.

After all these years, it was still Mary Ann, Bob and me who enjoyed each others' company. So when Thom died, I called Bob and naturally he called Mary Ann. She was lecturing in North Carolina. When she got the news, she called me right away.

"Hi, Sweetie. How are you doing?"

"Ugh," I sighed. "It's been a long haul, but it's finally over. I'm exhausted."

"Look, I'm changing my flights so I can come up there for a few days before I have to go back to work. Don't worry. I'll be your slave for the next two days. I'll do whatever you want. I'll cook, I'll clean, I'll play with the kids—I'm yours."

What a great feeling… First, the burden of waiting for Thom to die was lifted, and now someone who knew me and unconditionally loved me was going to show up and do anything I asked. Whatever I needed! I was overwhelmed with relief and gratitude.

Mary Ann came and we talked, cried, laughed and planned. She organized, did everything I asked and much more. She even volunteered to be the guardian of both Justine and Caitlin. When you are suddenly a single parent that idea of "Who will take my kids if I die?" becomes a heavy weight on your mind. Sarah could have done it, but Justine and Sarah would have had sparks flying on a daily basis. They are just too much alike.

Thinking of Sarah being a single Mom to three kids was too much. Mary Ann also loved my kids. Most importantly, she "got" Justine and Caitlin. Somehow, my two girls were similar to hers. Not only that, but she was an adolescent pediatrician and would be able to understand everything that they would need if—God forbid—they would actually be parentless before they were twenty-one.

We quickly went over an outline of my finances and what the most important things were that I wanted her to do for each of the girls in the near foreseeable future. Caitlin would remain at her school as a boarder and I made her promise that if Justine came to live with her that she would take Justine's horse too.

We stayed up late and then fell asleep in each other's arms. She left after the service, but I felt light-years ahead of where I was before she got here. God, I love her.

I've got to tell you that one of the weirdest and weightiest duties I had at this time was writing Thom's obituary. I knew it was coming. It had to be me. No one else could do it. I got out of it when Mom died. It fell to my oldest brother, Joe. He did it before she died. So when she passed, we just faxed it over to the paper.

I had forgotten all about it until a day or two after Thom died. If you think it's just a bunch of facts, try writing one for yourself. What would someone say about you? What would you want them to say? How do you want to be remembered? It's exhausting work fraught with emotional stress. My advice? Keep it simple.

More importantly, if you were to write one for yourself, like right now, it might change the way you conduct yourself from here on out. It certainly made me think. I won't have Thom around to assure me that I have done enough good in my life. I will have to know that for myself.

200

The Service

"Share the love you feel for me with everybody else.
Then the world will be such a better place." – *Jeff Drayton*

It was May 3, 2003. Some of that day moved in slow motion, and a few parts of it I don't recall at all. But what I do remember, I remember vividly.

Early that morning, I went down to the church to "smudge" the church with sage. I brought some of our orchids that were in bloom (my favorite was a dark plum lady slipper) with a few other plants. Thom had chosen H.O.R.S.E., a local horse rescue farm, as his choice for donations instead of condolence flowers. That early in the morning, the empty church was beautiful and still. Peaceful. Comforting. I went home knowing it was a fitting place for all of us to come together to say our farewells.

Justine went to the church ahead of me with her friends and our neighbors, Casey and Troy, along with their mother, Gail. Justine and Casey were each carrying their favorite stuffed animals. Justine's was, of course, a horse.

Caitlin and Sarah went together, probably after stopping for coffee.

All I remember about getting dressed was that I wanted to wear something spring-like, not dark. I wore a light chartreuse skirt with a matching purple and chartreuse knitted top. And I wore the amethyst pendant and earrings Thom had given me for our wedding anniversary.

I had this weird feeling that I was stuck in slow motion. Honestly, I don't know how long it took me to get ready, but it was a long time. Everyone in our family was already at the church, except for me.

Everything took so much longer to do than it should have. It felt like thirty minutes just to put my clothes on. Maybe it was because, subconsciously, I didn't want to go. But the next thing I remember is parking the car in the church parking lot.

I walked up to the church and there were all our friends, family, neighbors, the girls' teachers and their friends from school. There were Thom's friends and people I recognized from the program. There were my co-workers and doctor friends. They were filing from the parking lot, along the sidewalk and into the church.

It felt like I had just been let out of jail and there was a party going on. Everyone was here. Only it was weird since we were all here for Thom, without Thom, and because of Thom. I tried to get into the church. But there were people who I was so glad to see that I had to greet them. I was standing outside the front steps of the church, hugging and welcoming everyone.

Before I knew it a long line of people coming from the parking lot were queuing up to greet me on the way into the service. After all those days sequestered in my house, I was ecstatic to be standing in the sun and greeting all these wonderful people who I knew and loved.

Finally, after what must have been thirty minutes, Bonnie came over and urged me into the church. Perhaps I'd held up the service for a little too long. I was stuck like glue trying to get dressed and then I was stuck in a time warp outside the church. Death can change so many things.

My three girls and I, plus Justine's friend, Casey (and their stuffed animals) went in together as a family and sat in the front pews on the right.

Bonnie stood in the front of the church—what a comfort to see her standing there welcoming us. She looked official in her ceremonial white floor-length robes. She made the opening comments. We all sang together, prayed and heard the melodious voices of the *a cappella* group Femina Melodia. Everything sounded perfect in the church.

Then it was time for family remembrances. Whenever I have gone to services, this is the part I liked best, when members of the family tell stories about their loved one who has died. It always made the person more real to me.

Caitlin shared her thoughts first and walked up to the pulpit with a large book under her arm. She stood tall and official compared to those of us sitting in the pews.

Taking the book from under her arm, she placed it open to a marked page and started to read from Webster's dictionary! She proceeded to read the definition of death. As I recall, it stated that death was the end of life and that there was no more after death. Caitlin went on to debate the definition. She agreed with the death of the physical body, but it stopped there. She negated the idea of it being the end and "no more."

She spoke of the spiritual qualities of love: love having no ending. She also spoke about the fact that her Dad's genes were alive in her and her two sisters, that his genetic material would be living for quite some time to come. Her words were so beautiful—so Caitlin.

When it was Justine's turn, she marched right up to the pulpit. Bonnie put a big wooden box for Justine to stand on behind the pulpit so we could see her over the top of it. She looked out over the 250 people gathered there and she spoke in her usual confident fashion.

She talked about how her Dad died because he smoked and that was the wrong thing to do. However, he had done many good things in his life too, and she was choosing to remember those things about him instead. She spoke about him being a good father, a good husband and a person who helped other people with their problems. She added a few remembrances, then collected her papers and stepped down.

No one took a breath until she sat down. They were impressive speeches that made their Dad and Mom proud.

Now it was my turn. I was a little worried about what I was going to say since I had not written it down. After years of public speaking, I knew I gave my best deliveries when I didn't use note cards. Now, I was feeling a lot less confident than I ever had before. This was not the day I wanted that history of good deliveries to let me down. Most importantly, I didn't want to get too nostalgic or start crying. I had three or four important ideas to communicate and I didn't want the effect diluted by a bunch of tears.

I stood on the first step to the platform, in front of the pulpit. I had promised Thom that I would not ramble. However, I felt compelled to share the distilled essence of a thoughtful and powerful man. I had counted on the right words coming out in the way they were supposed to for the people who were there. As I looked at everyone gathered there, I took a deep breath and concentrated on being concise.

"Some of you may know Thom as Justine's Dad or Caitlin's Dad, perhaps as a friend or in some other fashion. But not everyone here knows that Thom was a therapist who helped people with their problems. More importantly, he was a therapist who specialized in death and dying.

"Given that background, I want you to know that he had the most fantastic death of anyone I have ever known. Believe me, as a physician, I have been around a lot of dying people. So I can say that with some assurance.

"Since he was diagnosed with cancer last year, but especially in these last four months when he knew he was going to die, he did a tremendous amount of soul-searching. So I am going to share with you three of his most important dying thoughts. This may make incredible sense to you or it may sound like nonsense. If you get it, it's for you. If you don't, don't worry, it's not for you. Anyway here goes.

"First thought from Thom:

> We should all constantly update
> our definitions of ourselves.

"What we were told about ourselves as children or at some previous time in our lives may not apply now. We need to take the time to reflect on our lives *now*—who we are, what we want to accomplish while we are on this earth, and where we are going.

"Do all the pieces come together to make the picture of who we think we are? Or want to be? If not, we need to change the pieces, change ourselves, or change the definition.

"Second thought from Thom:

It is never too late to be
as good as you can possibly be.

"Thom was someone who truly worked on bettering himself. What he did in these last three years, especially this last year, was remarkable. Since he was addicted to smoking cigarettes, I asked him what he thought, now that he was dying, about addictions. He said whatever fault a person has, addictions, anger or whatever—if they work on it and improve themselves it is their own personal key to spiritual success.

"You have the chance to improve yourself every day, even if you are dying, right up to the moment you die. He surely practiced this philosophy.

"Third thought from Thom:

It's 90% attitude.

"Meaning, how you choose to relate to your own life, whatever you get handed in your life, it's yours. You are not living a mistake. You got what you were supposed to get. It's yours to make sense of and learn from—or not.

"We don't have control over each event that happens in our lives, but we sure do have control about how we think about what happens to us. Having a good attitude and a sense of humor about it makes all the difference, especially to yourself. No one is a victim of their own life unless they choose to be.

"I promised Thom I wouldn't talk too long, so that's it. But Thom did want anyone who wanted to, to be able to tell their own stories or remembrances of him. So I invite you to say something if you feel that you can."

Half a minute is a long time in a situation like that, but I waited. I knew there were people present who wanted to say something and were probably trying to figure out how to say it.

Finally, my cousin, Bob, stood up and told some of the funniest camping stories I have ever heard. They were all about his camping with Thom, the girls and me. The whole congregation was roaring with laughter.

My niece had a barbeque sauce story. Thom's BBQ sauce was famous in our family, and it was so good that some of us were known to eat BBQ sauce sandwiches. Becka had the bravado to have a head-to-head tasting, her sauce versus Thom's. His was really the best, but hers was pretty darn good, so he wanted to know what her ingredients were. That's when she pulled out the store bought jar and read the label to him.

Other people had simpler sentiments about how they liked his easy smile, his sense of humor or his crazy socks, for which he was well known. One guy in the balcony said he loved Thom's Hawaiian shirts. He stood up to show everyone the Hawaiian shirt he had on, one that Thom had given him.

Bonnie closed the service with some soothing words about Thom and his life. She went on to say something about him looking down on us from above. With that Justine immediately piped up with, "But not while we are in the bathroom, right, Bonnie?" She was serious, yet the whole church could not help but shake with laughter.

We all laughed so easily, not only over this, but all the little vignettes that portrayed the unique, generous and humorous qualities of Thom. Things we would all miss…

Finally, it was quiet.

Caitlin played Pachelbel's Canon, the piece she played almost daily for her Dad. It was so familiar, yet somehow so different to hear it in a church. It was as if, in all that space, it could touch each person there before wafting upward, taking our thoughts and well-wishes to Thom, wherever he was.

The African drums were in dramatic contrast to Caitlin's playing. While the piano pulled at the heart strings and seemed to whisper goodbye, the drums announced a resounding arrival. You could feel it in your chest, a strong beating of anticipation and excitement. I guess that's the way it would be for Thom, a bittersweet goodbye and an outstanding welcome.

It was a fitting day for a man who led a great life and had a great death.

What was next for him?

I have my own ideas. Someday, I will be able to ask all my questions and have them answered. But as my brother, Pete, said, "By then, the answers won't matter anymore."

"You have to do me one really big favor," Thom asked me that first day, the day of his diagnosis.

Wanting to please him more than anything, I replied, "Sure, honey. You name it. What do you want?"

"You have to stop looking at me as if you're living with a dead man."

I never did live with a dead man—not even at the end.

Thom had always been the most alive man that I had ever known. But in his dying, he came even more to life. In his dying, he lived more than many people live in a lifetime. Maybe that's what all his "death and dying" expertise taught him. Maybe that is the truth we all seek, the meaning we all long for. Maybe that is the key to living—to be completely, irrevocably and unabashedly alive.

The End

So, now you have an idea of how good an ending can be. The "good death" secrets have been revealed to you here. Using all that dying has to offer to put your life in order before the end can add such meaning and satisfaction to your life. We are all going to have this experience. And you can make it as good as you want it to be.

I'd never known how good a death and its process could be until I learned that from Thom. It was an intensely intimate and gratifying experience. Now that time has gone by, I can look back without all the raw pain and impending loss. Thom's dying was a gift. It sounds weird, but this truth is coming from my core.

Now, the knowledge and understanding about the end of life and dying are mine in a way that wasn't possible before. This knowing is embroidered on my soul. It means more to me than I thought possible.

Like a deep tap root, I am planted in understanding. It defies description. I love this feeling. Here I am, formidable and fearless. Not only do I have no fear of death, but I am in awe of it. It compels me to live, love, celebrate, laugh and enjoy as much as possible. Humor is a powerful tool, and I have a million small ways to find happiness now.

How has Thom's death and dying affected me?

Many people have asked me this. The answer is complex and simple. It has affected every aspect of my life more than I can explain. Yet, what I can say is that because I refused to be a victim, shut down or be pissed off (for long), I was able to reap the benefits of Thom's lessons and remain positive. The profound changes that I have experienced, I never want to forfeit.

My mind is now lighter and more available for connections than ever before. I let go of the old "shoulds"—definitions of who I should be and what I should do, along with all the external definitions that were so restrictive of who I had become. I let them go. (Who made those up anyhow, and what where they doing in my subconscious?) Profound experiences clean them out like dusting away cobwebs.

There is nothing like a crisis to cut to the quick of what really matters in your life. The three lessons I learned from this experience are mindfulness, forgiveness and letting go.

(Oh and I learned to cook really well, almost as well as Thom. What fun! Who knew?)

Mindfulness

Stay here now.

Mindfulness, or staying in the now, takes a while to learn. It is a discipline of the mind. It gets easier the more you do it though.

When I was able to stay in the here and now (not thinking about what had been or worrying about what was to come), I felt amazingly calm. It was like a mental vacation.

When I returned to my everyday thinking, I often found that my priorities had shifted significantly. What I thought had to be done as soon as I got home could to be put off until tomorrow. I could make room for myself and reduce my pressure and anxiety.

There are two ways people can increase their mindfulness, even when they feel stuck in a stressful position.

The first is to stay still and simply breathe. Concentrate on inhaling for a few seconds, then exhaling for a few seconds, repeating this until they can feel themselves settling down. This meditation is simple and it works.

The second is to stay present in your body, be aware of where you are and how you are sitting. Pull your thoughts into the here and now through your senses and awareness, not staying on any one thought too long. There are many classes, CDs and internet resources to help with this journey.

Meditation's ability to help the pained mind or soul is immense. This is a powerful life tool that the girls and I shared with Thom through chanting, drumming and singing. Caitlin did this too with her piano playing.

Forgiveness

In the end, this is all that matters.

Hurt or pain is intensely personal. When it reaches a certain level, all you can think of is getting away from it.

Thom's alcohol addiction was so hurtful to me that it made me want him permanently out of my life, just to avoid ever feeling that degree of pain again. It was an easy solution, just get rid of him, and the pain would be gone. My anger was enough to throw him away, not even caring where he would have landed. Where would any of us land? Then what?

Forgiveness is not like a simple light switch—either it's there or it's not. Instead, it's more like a dimmer that can go from barely perceptible to full brightness.

Looking back, I have no idea how I opted for forgiveness. I had no real experience with it before this. My "forgiveness light" was pretty dim for some time, but I felt better as it brightened. My hurt eased and hope squeezed in, which helped make the light brighter.

I was sure that I would never feel the same toward Thom, but perhaps I would feel a different satisfaction or contentment grow between us.

Forgiveness was the hardest lesson for me and that's why I am so proud I learned it. It is an immensely powerful experience. When I chose to forgive my sister, Regina, it opened us both up to reconnecting. We now have the greatest sisterly love, and I almost missed it!

Letting Go

It is going the way it should.

Our lives are based on what our parents, grandparents, religion and cultural norms have instilled in us. These, along with our life experiences, make up our Life Instruction Manuals. We live the way we do because we are doing "the right thing," the way things are supposed to be. Along we go until we hit a landmine.

Cancer and death were what blew my world apart. Everything in my life changed: the rules, my work, my family, my friends, how I ate, slept, what I spoke about, and even what I thought was important all changed.

One of the biggest turning points was when Thom decided no more chemo, no more treatments. We all shifted into dying mode and everything changed. Up until then, letting go had been a trickle by comparison, but now it was an open floodgate.

Before that day, I spent a lot of time trying to reconcile cancer with our everyday life, trying to make sense of cancer. It sounds stupid now, but that is what my logical mind was trying to do. That day marked the beginning of letting go.

When I realized that all of my questions had no answers, I had to accept that I was at a standstill. I let go of trying to make sense of everything. I let go of the way I thought things should be or could have been. I let go of resentment. This made way for the transformation of my thinking and my life.

I eventually realized Thom was on his own journey and I had no control or say over it. I was not responsible for him on this journey. I couldn't fix it. Or maybe, after all, it didn't need fixing.

The bottom line is nobody knows enough about death when they are in the middle of it. Each of us has or will find out the realities of death in time. It is the non-negotiable end. It will take who we have known and loved and be gone.

This memoir is just one example of how it was. There will be analogies to you or your loved one's death. Take any idea or thought that works for you and run with it. There is only one rule: Do not pretend death is not going to happen.

Here are some of the things I now know about myself.

I will tell my loved ones that I love them. Often.

I will keep champagne on ice and break it out to celebrate life's many accomplishments.

I will not pretend death is not coming.

I will not leave my family unprepared for death.

I will remain open and vulnerable to death and life.

I will not shut down, shut out or shut up.

I will love all that I am able and it will not stop when I die.

These things I know. I know them for sure.

Goodbye now, my dear. I have been dreaming about the words to leave you with. Here they are:

If death has the capacity
to transform life in all ways,
including redefining yourself
for the better and becoming as great
as you can possibly be,
challenge yourself to keep
a positive attitude everyday

work through pain
get a real doctor
show up
own up
listen up
love it up
and live it up

Why wait for death?

Author's Note

A few parting words for you...

Everyone who goes through cancer or has an impending death needs an advocate. If you ever find yourself going through this, know that this is a time when you need help. The diagnosis, chemo, surgery, radiation or whatever, this process is infinitely easier if you have a family doctor on your team.

The author Stephen Levine, who wrote *Who Dies? An Investigation of Conscious Living and Conscious Dying*, defines the family doctor as one of the most important advocates a dying person can have. They are someone who knows medicine, but they also know you. Your family doctor can guide you through the landmines and help you arrive where and how you want.

Do not underestimate this relationship. If you have one, use them. If you don't have one, find one. Make an appointment to discuss your options and perspectives on cancer and death, and do it before the end, so that they can help you along the way.

Steve, a long-time patient of mine, died a while back. He and Betsy, his wife, involved me in his whole dying process. Not long after his death, Betsy showed up at the office crying, heartbroken and sobbing uncontrollably. Wendy looked out to the waiting room to see who was so distraught and seeing Betsy brought her right into an exam room.

From where I was in another room, I could hear her loudly crying and I quickly went to her. As we sat holding hands, she screamed about how awful this phase was without Steve.

"You know," she said. "You know how bad it is."

"It sure is," I answered softly, remembering how some days seemed so overwhelming.

She said it hit her while walking their dog and she burst out screaming and crying on the sidewalk. Neighbors came out of their houses to see if there was anything they could do for her. She was inconsolable and didn't know what to do to make herself feel better, until she thought about coming to my office. So she came.

"This is where I feel good. This is my sanctuary. You know me and Steve. You know me intimately and I always feel good here. So I had to come here."

This was my finest compliment, but the point is: a good family doctor knows everything is connected in your body and in your life. They can help you navigate through it all. Get one.

Acknowledgements

Despite the writing of this book being "on me," it was definitely a group effort, and I'd like to take a moment to thank all of those people who helped make this book a reality.

Thom of course gave me the title, the story and the initial idea.

Bonnie Bardot suggested that instead of trying to write a book, why not just tell my story? "Storytelling is how we learn best," she said.

Cindy Maddox took one hundred individual slips of paper with notes on them and wove them into the first storyline.

Wendy Santos, my office manager and friend, steadied me at work, read and encouraged my writing, and helped me to survive in oh-so-many ways.

My daughters, Caitlin and Justine, were soul support and inspiration, and my step-daughter, Sarah, was great support too while she was here and when she returned home. (She also wrote a play along the same lines.)

My sister-in-law (more sister and less in-law), Debbie Bette, was there every step of the way and helped in so many different ways, from Costco runs and a vacation in the red convertible, to simply listening over the hundreds of miles that we have walked together.

My BFFs, Kathleen Lord, Helen Chittum, Lisa Golyembioski and Eileen Flint, who read, critiqued and supported me all the way to print.

Obviously, all the people mentioned in this book were a big help.

And lastly I'd like to thank my patients, many of whom encouraged me with their thoughts and stories.

About the Author

Marianne Bette is a family physician in Southbury, Connecticut, the town where she was born and raised. She is also a clinical professor at the medical schools of the University of Connecticut, Quinnipiac University and the University of Vermont.

She went to Loyola University in Chicago, and attended medical school at the University of Southern California in Los Angeles. For 18 years she lived and worked in the "high desert" of Palmdale and Lancaster, CA, before moving back to Southbury 17 years ago.

Marianne has three daughters who she's very proud of.

The oldest, her stepdaughter Sarah, lives in California with her three children and her husband, who is a chef.

Her daughter, Caitlin, is in her last year of UConn medical school and is going into Family Practice.

Justine, the youngest, is in her third year of college at Warren Wilson College in Asheville, NC, and is studying to become an equine-facilitated psychotherapist.

While Marianne never anticipated becoming an author, as many writers know, sometimes there's a story that just won't let you go until it's written. When Marianne's husband, Thom, asked her to write this book, she never thought she would. Twelve years later, it is finally seeing the light of day.

Her hope is that, in reading it, you reconnect to the people and ideals that are most important to you in living a fulfilling life.

Clockwise from top left, all prior to Thom's diagnosis:

Marianne and Thom enjoying Thanksgiving in 2001

Caitlin at 10 or 11 years old

Justine and Sarah

Thom preparing Thanksgiving dinner

Top: The family together, when Caitlin won National History Day, June 2002

Middle, left: Thom and Sarah, August 2002

Middle, right: Marianne and Thom, Thanksgiving 2002

Top: Thom in his Prepared Minds t-shirt Caitlin had made, with Justine, Christmas 2002

221

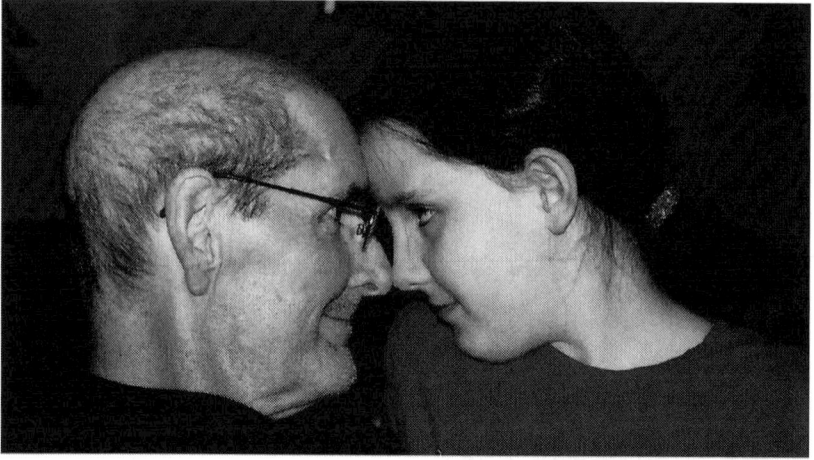

Top: Thom and Justine in one of Marianne's favorite photos, early January 2003

Middle: Thom with the tapestry in the bedroom, late February 2003. Marianne had a strict rule of "No dogs on the bed," but Thom wanted Sam to visit, so that's what he got!

Bottom: Thom and Caitlin, snuggling in bed, March 2003

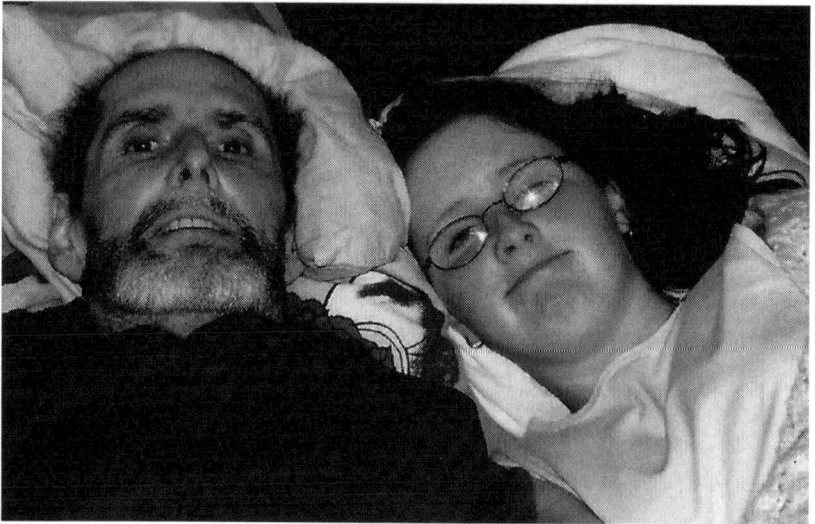